THE
DINNER
CHURCH
HANDBOOK

THE
DINNER
CHURCH
HANDBOOK

*A Step-by-Step Recipe
for Reaching Neighborhoods*

Verlon Fosner

 Seedbed

Unless otherwise noted, Scripture quotations are taken from the Holy Bible, New Living Translation, copyright 1996, 2004. Used by permission of Tyndale House Publishers, Inc., Wheaton, Illinois 60189. All rights reserved.

Scripture quotations marked ESV are taken from The Holy Bible, English Standard Version. ESV® Permanent Text Edition® (2016). Copyright © 2001 by Crossway Bibles, a publishing ministry of Good News Publishers.

Scripture quotations marked KJV are taken from the Holy Bible, King James Version, Cambridge, 1796.

Printed in the United States of America

Cover design by Strange Last Name
Page design by PerfecType, Nashville, Tennessee

Fosner, Verlon.
   The dinner church handbook : a step-by-step recipe for reaching neighborhoods / Verlon Fosner. — Frankin, Tennessee : Seedbed Publishing, ©2017.

      vi, 162 ; 21 cm.
      Includes bibliographical references (pages147-161)

      ISBN 9781628243925 (paperback : alk. paper)
      ISBN 9781628243932 (Mobi)
      ISBN 9781628243949 (ePub)
      ISBN 9781628243956 (uPDF)

      1. Evangelistic work--United States.   2. Dinners and dining--Religious aspects--Christianity.   3. Hospitality--Religious aspects--Christianity.   4. Church development, New--United States.   5. Westminster Community Church (Shoreline, Wash.)   I. Title.

BV3790 .F678 2017   269/.2   2017941524

SEEDBED PUBLISHING
Franklin, Tennessee
Seedbed.com

CONTENTS

INTRODUCTION

A Challenge—an Opportunity—a Call

The American church is waning. With fifty-three thousand people deciding to stop attending church every week,[1] eighty churches closing every week,[2] and fifty pastors leaving the ministry every day,[3] it is obvious that something is downshifting. In fact, only 30 percent of the population now attends church,[4] and only 15 percent of churches are reporting growth.[5] This is an unusual missional situation for us that has never been seen before in the United States. And yet, most Christian leaders are spending the majority of their efforts running programs and worship services for the "already gathered." Alton Garrison, assistant general superintendent of the Assemblies of God, reported, "Our research shows that 80 percent of our denomination's members believe that church is to provide a place where Christians can share God's love with one another."[6] This is not a healthy attitude for the people who are supposed to be engaged in the greatest rescue project this world has ever seen: Christianity.

The Challenge

The church in America has a sociological problem. Throughout US history, churches have predominantly located in middle- and upper-class neighborhoods, serving those who can afford the expensive proclamation church model that the reformers invented. Missionary and church planter Alan Johnson observed that Christianity seems to be following a missiology that locates its churches and efforts in circumstances, not of poverty, but of wealth; not of oppression, but of freedom; not where non-Christians are, but where Christian's are.[7] This prevailing assumption has left American churches under-practiced in their ability to endear themselves to one-third of the population, those who live in sore neighborhoods. Their impoverished and isolated sociology makes it unlikely that the poor will ever feel comfortable in their middle- to upper-class Sunday-morning gatherings, or even feel the need to shape moral ideas when they are struggling to make rent and buy food. Their world is a very different one—a survivalist one—even though they live just a couple of blocks away from our sanitized churches.

The Opportunity

A simple study of the Gospels reveals that Christ spent much of his time with poor people; that should speak something very loud to us. Historically, the church's greatest relevance was garnered by the way they lifted the poor in their cities. Yet, present church leaders continue to assume that most of our nation is composed of middle- and upper-class people. It would serve us well to pause and remember that a lower third exists in America too. In fact, many economists are reporting that a thinning of the middle class is occurring, and an increased number of Americans are slipping into the lower-third income bracket.[8] As frustrating as this is for many of our countrymen, it widens a large opportunity for the church. Nothing will give a church influence any faster than reaching for "the least of these" who live surprisingly close to them, and in large numbers (see Matthew 25:40).

The Call

Throughout history, whenever the church got serious about reaching the sore populations, it got serious about the dinner church approach. In fact, this was the manner of church that best defined the apostolic era. Reviving the ancient dinner church vision opens a very big door for church planting in sore neighborhoods. To put an apostolic ear to the ground is to hear these challenged populations inviting the church to be with them. I propose that we say yes to these invitations and start doing church for them in their neighborhoods in a way they can embrace.

THE HISTORIC DINNER CHURCH

Revisiting the Ancient Agape Feast:
A Vision for Church Expansion

The church as we know it today did not always look like this—people gathering on Sunday mornings, sitting in straight rows, singing with a worship band, listening to a speaker for thirty minutes, bowing their heads for a benediction, and then streaming out in the exact way they came in. This is not how our founders celebrated their faith. Rather than a proclamation-based church, the first church was actually a dinner church. While the proclamation-based churches have done many great things for worshippers through the centuries, the dinner church offered a very different spiritual experience. The great writer and theologian Henri Nouwen once stated, "If there is any concept worth restoring to its original depth and evocative potential, it is the concept of hospitality."[1]

The concept of divine hospitality dates back to the Old Testament, when God revealed his presence on the earth through numerous sacred meals. With that as the backdrop of history, it is little wonder that Jesus used a meal strategy to invite people into the kingdom of God. It is also understandable why the first church followed the ways of their Master and used dinnertimes to establish their presence throughout the Mediterranean basin. One would be hard-pressed to find New Testament evidence of any church gathering that did not meet around a shared meal. The good news was an easy message to deliver when served in the atmosphere of an agape meal, in which all manner of men and women were included.

As wonderful an experience as the dinner church provided, however, it did not last. By the beginning of the fourth century, the dinner church was eclipsed by a different vision altogether. In retrospect, it might be that more was lost than we have imagined. There might be value in this day, even two thousand years later, to reconsider the ancient agape meal setting and the warm, inclusive gospel it promoted.

The Long-Standing Sacred Meal Tradition

God's Table. From the beginning, God showed up at mealtime. The very first recorded words that God spoke to Adam referred to all the trees in the garden from which Adam was to *eat* (Gen. 2:16–17).[2] Dr. Robert Stallman, a professor of Old Testament studies at Northwestern University, wrote, "Eating is at the center of Eden."[3] Shared meals are well established in the Old Testament and serve as the occasion for recognizing a new level of divine relationship.[4] We see this relational intent clearly in Exodus when God called Moses and the elders to come to Mount Sinai to ratify the covenant, and while they were there, God provided a divinely catered meal that revealed an unprecedented level of fellowship with God.[5] We see it again in Deuteronomy 29:5–6, just before Israel's entrance into Canaan, where the text recounts how God had "spread a table" for them in the wilderness for forty years.[6] The psalmist referred to that same truth in Psalm 78:19 by asking a rhetorical question, "Can God furnish a table in the wilderness?" (KJV).[7] The prophets also crafted the imagery of table fellowship with God in Isaiah 25:6–8, and promoted it as the sublime experience to be sought.[8] Dr. Stallman concluded that the very axis of Yahweh's relationship with Israel would come to expression every time God's people shared a meal or feast.[9]

Presence. The sacred meals of the Abrahamic covenant, the Sinai covenant, Gideon's covenant, and the many repeating feasts of the Mosaic law had less to do with a covenantal signature and more to do with evidence that God was among them and proving it by sitting down at a sacred meal with them. Professor John Michael Perry of Cardinal Stritch University wrote, "According to the Law of Moses, a shared meal was one of the ways by which God assured Israel of covenant friendship and access to divine blessing."[10] The idea of God's presence at a sacred meal permeated Israel's mind-set; they understood these mealtimes to reassure them that God was with them and intended to pour favor and blessing upon them.[11]

Daily Life. The divine table fellowship idea spilled over into Israel's daily life. "The practice of hospitality in the ancient near East, going back long before Jesus' time and continuing to today, involved the notion that the guest in someone's tent or house was sacrosanct, treated with respect."[12] *Ragamuffin Gospel* author Brennan Manning stated, "The ancient Jewish practice of inviting someone for dinner meant, 'come to my *mikdash me-at*,' the miniature sanctuary of my dining room table, where we will celebrate the most sacred and beautiful experience that life affords—friendship."[13] Hospitality was a divinely inspired activity for ancient peoples, and it always involved shared meals and validated the dignity of guests.[14] The people who were most affected by Yahweh were drawn to value the sacredness of mealtime.

Jesus' Meal Strategy

Healing and Eating. It was against the Old Testament backdrop of sacred meal symbolism that Jesus extended table fellowship, even to those who were notorious sinners.[15] In fact, Jesus employed a very intentional dinner strategy during his three-year ministry. New Testament scholar John Dominic Crossan suggested that to watch Jesus during an average day would reveal him doing two things repeatedly: healing and eating.[16] Correspondingly, the visual art of Jesus in the pre-Constantinian era reveals that the two most common elements of his life were shared meals and healed lives.[17] Jesus clearly employed a dinner strategy in his ministry; in fact, it was this practice that created many conflicts for him. In Luke 15:1–2, Jesus angered his critics because he extended a welcome to sinners and their friends to join him at his table.[18] N. T. Wright, another New Testament scholar, said, "Most writers now agree that eating with sinners was one of the most characteristic and striking marks of Jesus' regular activity."[19] It is quite apparent that Jesus' controversial dinners were an intentional and prominent feature of his prophetic mission to Israel.[20] Dr. Julian Hills, associate professor of New Testament and Christian origins at Marquette University, said that Jesus intended his use of the open dinner table to be a central feature in the Christian tradition he was instilling in his followers.[21] Jesus' dinner approach had some practical value, as most people worked during the day and were only available at dinnertime to engage in a spiritual conversation. But there was more than mere practicality involved in Jesus' use of mealtime. It is clear that Jesus viewed these dinners as an invitation to faith and repentance.[22] A great example of the salvation power of a dinner is when Jesus sat at Zaccheus's table. It is likely that Jesus, as usual, spoke of the kingdom and God's offer of forgiveness for everyone, and this offer of God's love is what touched and changed Zaccheus's heart.[23]

Jesus' Controversial Suppers. Where did Jesus tell many of his parables? We may reasonably assume that the contexts in which Jesus usually recited his parables was during his controversial suppers.[24] In fact, Jesus seemingly crafted the parables found in Luke 15 to defend his practice of welcoming sinners to his dinners.[25] Most New Testament readers have acknowledged that Jesus was a master storyteller, but perhaps they have not imagined the dinner setting as the place those stories were told. One can see how these parables would captivate a room of listeners as they sat around tables of food. In fact, many of the parables were food and feast related because of the setting and the invited guests. One feast-oriented instruction that Jesus gave at a dinner is found in Luke 14:12–14, where he told hosts to invite the poor and those who cannot pay back. The most famous feast-oriented parable, the parable of the great feast (Matthew 22:1–14), was consciously drawn from a story in Palestinian oral tradition of a tax collector named Bar Maayan, who gave a banquet for the city counselors; when they refused to come, he gave orders that the poor should come and eat the food.[26] These stories about inviting the poor to meals, banquets, and end-time feasts reveal that Jesus saw the kingdom in terms of feasting.[27] Another interesting story that intensifies the great importance of hospitality, found in Matthew 25, is about separating sheep from goats. This story ends by opening the door to heaven only to the sheep—the group that cared for the sick, visited the imprisoned, and invited the poor to their tables.[28] Jesus eating with sinners and telling his stories about "the least of these" (Matthew 25:45) became the memory and template that inspired the ways and means of the first church.

A Vision for the First Followers

The Passover's New Vision. Jesus gathered his disciples for one final meal before his arrest, which just happened to be the Passover meal. Though the idea that it was a Passover meal has received some criticism, there can be little debate in light of Mark 14:12–14 that John Mark assumed it was a Passover meal.[29] It is also likely that John Mark viewed Jesus as the Passover Lamb.[30] When Jesus lifted up the bread and the wine and attributed them to himself, it spoke volumes to the disciples—Jesus was the Lamb that takes away the sins of the world. Then, when Jesus instructed them to share that same meal often, and to remember him as they did it, it is very unlikely that they would have interpreted his words to only apply to the bread and the cup, as in modern church practice. We need only to look at what they did following Jesus' ascension to know that they embraced the vision of the whole meal that Jesus gave them that night. After all, they had watched Jesus' dinner strategy for three years obviously, they understood the vision he was casting during this final Passover. In other words, the disciples were given a call to eat dinner together with sinners often and talk about Jesus. This was to be the manner of Christ's new church—a dinner church. The Judaic celebration of the Passover was superseded by the Lord's Supper meal.[31] The disciples caught the vision, and their gatherings were now done in the likeness of the Master's, around tables at dinnertime.

Slaves, Sinners, and Tax Collectors. There was something very winsome about these dinner settings. Professor and pastor Ben Witherington said, "Christian meals, including the Lord's Supper, had elements that worked against the prevailing hierarchy and stratification of society and were different from early Jewish meals."[32] There was a profoundly egalitarian dimension to these dinners.[33] The meal vision that Jesus instilled exemplified the radical leveling that the *kerygma* (preaching) proclaimed: everyone would be served equally.[34] Jesus' life and his continual welcoming of slaves, sinners, and despised tax collectors made it impossible to imagine that Jesus would champion any meal setting except an inclusive, "come one, come all" dinner table. This, then, reveals why Jesus selected the Passover meal for his vision launch.

The Rescue Continues. The historic theme of the Passover meal was all about the rescue of slaves. "The Mishnah explicitly requires that every one of the participants in the Passover meal sees oneself as 'one who has come out of Egypt.'"[35] The notion of the rescue of slaves was indelibly welded to the Passover meal. When Jesus took that moment to launch his vision for the manner of his church, he forcefully connected his meals to the rescue of the lost and needy. According to John Michael Perry, "Unless we understand the steps involved in the ritual by which God extended table fellowship to Israel through the communion sacrifice, we will not be able to appreciate fully the significance of table fellowship in the prophetic teaching of Jesus."[36] The first step of the Passover ritual was the killing of an animal, followed by the transformation of the gift by fire from an earthly to a heavenly condition, then the translation of the gifts to the heavenly sanctuary to signify the worshipper's desire for peace from God, and finally, God's acceptance of the gifts, as evidenced by the table fellowship.[37] Every serious Hebrew attending a Passover celebration would be led through these steps as the evening progressed, and it would culminate with the invitation to sit with God at the table of fellowship and receive his blessing and favor.

The meaning of the Passover table was profound: God has rescued us and now sits to eat with us. Amazingly, Jesus instructed his followers to take that same table and its rich meaning of rescue and divine inclusion to the commoners, the sinners, the lost, the poor, the lonely, and the despised. The backdrop of the Passover is the greatest theological explanation for the dinner church, and from that spiritual history Christ instilled his dinner vision.

A Dinner Church

Beyond Breaking Bread. Within a couple of months of Christ's ascension, there developed a regular weekly common meal held in the house churches. Dr. Julian Hills stated that the common meals practiced by early Christian communities are in direct response to the legacy of Jesus.[38] In the first two chapters of the book of Acts, the followers are going from house to house, sitting with their neighbors, breaking bread, and talking about Jesus. Whenever we see the phrase "breaking bread," there is a larger event being communicated, and is likely a technical term for the whole meal.[39] This understanding opens up many scriptures to support the developing meal strategy of the first church all through the book of Acts and beyond. In fact, many New Testament verses make more sense when applied to a dinner table. A great example is the debate over whether or not it is permissible to eat certain foods, especially meat (see Romans 14:2–3). The conflict was intense precisely because Christians were worshipping around the same tables at which they ate, and the meat in question was sitting right in front of them.

Feasting with Neighbors. Many obvious references to the dinner church movement require no explanation. In Acts 20, young Eutychus fell from the upper window as Paul preached right through the dinner hour. After Paul prayed over him, the believers all went back inside and finally ate, even though it was past midnight. In 1 Corinthians 11, we see the diverse nature of the dinner church: Paul rebuked the Christians for hoarding the food and leaving the poor who had been invited unfed and unwelcomed to the table. While that was a negative chapter in the dinner church history, it reveals the meal commingled with the inclusion of the poor. One of the later references that prove the dinner church practice is found in Jude 12, where the agape feasts and the Lord's Supper were celebrated together during evening meals.[40] These suppers were called "love feasts" (ESV) because each time believers met for this meal, Jesus' command to love one's neighbor as oneself was recalled and observed.[41] Interestingly, Jude is a penultimate book, which means that, unlike Paul's epistles, which were written to specific places, such as Corinth and Ephesus, it was to be circulated and read among many churches in the region. Accordingly, Jude assumed that the agape meal was the typical manner of those numerous gatherings; the dinner church was going strong on Sunday evenings in Bithynia in AD 113.[42]

Mark's Mother. One of the little-talked-about but significant proofs of the dinner church is the book of Mark. In the second century, Papias made it clear that Mark was not an eyewitness to the life of Christ; he was too young. He was, however, an interpreter of Peter.[43] Mark's mother had an upstairs flat where she hosted gatherings that were, in fact, the very earliest Christian gatherings.[44] Mark most likely became Peter's interpreter in those weekly meetings, where they met for dinner and listened to Peter recount the stories of Christ.

Liminality. One of the values that emanated from the dinner church practice was the commitment to include "the least of these" (see Matthew 25:34–40). The defining characteristic of the early church was the way they opened up their homes and lives to strangers and outcasts. When these early disciples shared meals with others, the presence of God and his kingdom was revealed and reflected.[45] According to Professor Christine Pohl of Asbury

Theological Seminary, early Christian writers claimed that by sharing meals with people of different social and ethnic backgrounds, they proved the truth of the Christian faith.[46] Strangers and outcasts were a natural fit for the emerging dinner churches not only because the marginalized needed food and community, but also because they were the primary group that Jesus sought when he was on earth. Dinner churches found Christological alignment naturally.

Much is said about liminality in modern theological circles. Anthropologist Victor Turner stated, "Liminal persons are neither here nor there; they are betwixt and between and slip through the network of classifications in cultural space."[47] Liminality is a helpful term in understanding the people whom dinner churches seemed to embrace so instinctively. The first Christians, like Christ himself, seemed quite comfortable with liminality. In fact, they provided a stable place for people who were otherwise "betwixt and between." Pohl believed that the most potent setting for Christian hospitality was in the shared meals that occurred in the overlap of private and public space.[48] That is the exact social location in which the dinner churches of old existed; from that location they met loneliness and poverty with open arms in the name of Jesus the Christ.

Abundance. Another value that emanated from the dinner church practice was the image of abundance. It became a rule of hospitality that an abundance of food, more than could be eaten by the attendees, shaped not only the biblical stories of loaves and fishes, but also the agape meals.[49] Christian hospitality had a distinctive quality to it that offered a generous welcome, without concern for the host.[50] Dr. Pohl stated, "In the Christian hospitality tradition, most writers did not assume scarcity; they assumed that the problem was with distribution. They argued that if people shared their surplus with those in need, there would be enough for everyone."[51] This sheds light on why members of the Acts church would give such great amounts of wealth and even sell property, so as to provide food for their tables that would be shared with the poor. It has been suggested that the early Christians viewed giving to the poor as lending to God, knowing that he would repay the debt. In this way, humankind worked with God in the divine expression of abundance. Beyond that, the image of abundance had a mysterious and miraculous side to it. Interestingly, modern practitioners speak of always having enough food to serve the hungry no matter how many people show up, like a mysterious connection with the miracles of bread and fish.[52] I would propose that the image of abundance is important to God and spills forward to this very day.

Immanence. The dinner church practice naturally and intentionally created the expectation of immanence. It would be wrong to assume that gathering for dinner was merely a church service style. For the first followers it was the way they embraced the promise of God's presence among them. "The Qumran texts bear witness that in some quarters in early Judaism, Messianic hopes were high, and meals were seen as one essential part of the *koinonia* that one would share with the Anointed One."[53] In other words, though they predated Christ's arrival on the earth by a couple of decades, their meals were rich with anticipation of the Messiah's presence. Julian Hill asserted that the Qumran community, like the early church, saw these meals as an anticipation of the final banquet with Christ in heaven, another step toward that moment.[54] Beyond those early Qumran worshippers, the early church connected their fellowship meals to the promises of God and the presence of Christ.[55] The early disciples experienced numerous connections between suppertime and Christ's presence. For instance, the meal of bread and fish that Jesus gave to the disciples on the shore after Jesus' resurrection (John 21) signifies not only the appearance of the risen Jesus, but his abiding presence at his called mealtimes.[56] Then there is the time in Luke 24, where Jesus met the two on the road to Emmaus. When he sat to eat dinner with them and broke the bread, their eyes were opened (vv. 30–31). These instances and more led those first followers to understand that any Christian supper was a sign that Jesus was still among them.[57] I imagine that Christ's final words, "I am with you always, even to the end of the age" (Matt. 28:20) rang the loudest in their hearing as they sat together at their agape feasts.

Natural Evangelism. Another result of the dinner church practice was effective and natural evangelism. The practice of meals, which began with Jesus and continued throughout the New Testament era, was an ongoing feature that significantly helped the cause of evangelism right up to and beyond the end of the Roman Empire.[58] Christine Pohl went so far as to state that the growth in the earliest churches was wholly dependent on the meals and hospitality of the believers.[59] The agape meal was perhaps the primary manner of evangelism for the early church. There remained a natural draw for sinners to sit with saints, and while eating together, they talked about Jesus. Those who gathered around those tables might have been sinners, but they were redeemed sinners.[60] Something wonderful, unexplainable, and transformative occurred to the most unlikely of people in these dinner settings.

The Mark of Leadership. It is worth pointing out that the ability to serve dinners and engage in hospitality became a stated requirement for leadership. This is seen clearly in 1 Timothy 3:2 and Titus 1:8, where hospitality is listed as a special mark of fitness for leadership within the household of God (KJV).[61] Obviously, that mark of leadership would not be important unless the practice of the group was that of a dinner church and focused on the needs of the poor. Dr. Pohl maintained that hospitality was not optional for those early Christians.[62] This was a dinner church, and its people were called to reenact divine hospitality as their Christian expression.

The Dinner Vision Continues

By the beginning of the second century, the leading edge of the church had moved into many multicultural cities and situations. What began with the Jews was now as much the domain of Greek and Roman people. With three primary cultures making up the populace of most cities in the New Testament, there is a need to understand how they blended together into one workable culture and created space for the meal-based church.

Oikos. The initial social foundation for all of the groups of the Mediterranean basin was the household. "The idea of the household as a unit of society that might be compared with republic or kingdom was familiar."[63] Yet their version of a household was larger than we would expect, and it included servants, day laborers, and tenants installed on an owner's property.[64] The New Testament word *oikos* can mean "household," but it can also refer to a whole clan or tribe of people who have descended from a common ancestor.[65] A household was a larger number of people numbering from dozens to even hundreds. The birthing church found natural space in these cities by meeting in the larger rooms of people's homes. When the New Testament uses the phrase "the church in one's house," it denotes the meeting of a larger body of Christians through the hospitality of a particular household, and included celebrations surrounding communal meals.[66] A whole church may have reached forty to forty-five people. The church at Troas commonly met on Saturday at sunset, while most of the rest met on Sunday evenings at dinnertime.[67] Professor Elizabeth Newman of Baptist Theological Seminary said that when Christians gathered around both the Word and the table, a place of hospitality was created that was at once *oikos* (household) and *polis* (public).[68] The city cultures of the second century viewed society as having two realms, the household setting and public settings. These dinner churches created a societal setting somewhere between those social poles. According to Newman, the *ekklesia* exploded the strict dichotomy between *polis* and *oikos*; God's *oikonomia* became tangible in a unique space and a unique public setting in its own right.[69] In other words, a new kind of community formed, something that Roman, Greek, and Jewish cultures had never seen.

A Different Dinner. A cultural practice that these blended cities created was a variety of secular guilds and evening fellowships. Wayne Meeks, Woolsey professor emeritus of biblical studies at Yale University, revealed that "the early Roman Empire witnessed a luxuriant growth of clubs, guilds, and associations of all sorts."[70] The Greeks brought their symposiums into the cultural milieu, which was a banquet that ended with a philosophical reading or speech. Interestingly, John 13 portrays the Passover meal as a symposium banquet with Jesus' words of institution cast like the philosophical speech at the end of the dinner. This was probably done as a missiological effort to relate John's words to readers who did not understand Passover history.[71]

The Romans brought their evening fellowship tradition too, the famous *convivas.* These often turned into drinking events in which the wives were removed after dinner so the harder drinking could begin and the prostitutes could be brought in. The Jewish people also brought their evening meal traditions into the cultural mix, but with some adjustments. Sometimes these were referred to as *berakoth,* or "benedictions," and were based on the prayers that opened and ended the dinner. The Didache included some of these *berakoth,* and other sources included some that dated back to the Babylonian exile. In the prayer book called *Berakoth,* chapter 8 reveals that the table customs of the Jews were largely modeled on those of the Romans.[72] This citing shows the blending of the cultures that was occurring in these cities and affecting the dinner fellowships and the nightlife.

The dinner church found it easy to function amid the many secular guilds and fellowships and, in fact, established itself as a unique fellowship experience. "The Church had qualities unparalleled in the ancient world. Nowhere else would you find slaves and masters, Jews and Gentiles, rich and poor, engaged in table fellowship and showing a real love for one another."[73] The rest of the guilds and fellowships gathered around a similar social status and like occupations. This new dinner church cut across hierarchical and socioeconomic lines, which was shocking to the many other dinner clubs; they were more inclusive in terms of social stratification than were the other associations.[74] However, the opponents of Christianity started to identify the Christian groups with the *convivas* and clubs that sponsored uncontrolled gatherings and lumped them all together as "seedbeds of immorality."[75] This "guilt by association" campaign became no small challenge for the dinner church.

A Dinner Service Worth Fighting For. One of the great champions of the dinner church in the second century was Tertullian. It must be noted that we have such a large amount of material about Tertullian and the church in Carthage, North Africa, because of the mounting criticism against the dinner church vision. "In about AD 197, Tertullian wrote *Apologia* in North Africa, defending the Love Feast, or Agape Meal, against pagan slanders. The more ascetical the Church became, the more concern there was about the potential bad witness of the Agape."[76] Tertullian defended his agape meals by saying that worship, fellowship, and feasting were all carried out under the Father's eye. The lowly, the needy, and the sick were shown particular consideration.[77] Regarding another of Tertullian's responses, Ben Witherington wrote, "Tertullian mentions that the participants are asked to . . . sing to God [sing a psalm] . . . This is used as a sort of Breathalyzer test! One must suppose that if they started slurring their speech as they cranked up the volume of 'Amazing Grace,' then everyone knew they had had too much wine."[78] While that paints a humorous picture, it had serious implications for Tertullian, who was trying to prove that the dinner church was, indeed, controlling themselves and worthy of respect. Again Tertullian defended his agape feast by saying, "We go forth from the feast not like troops of mischief doers nor bands of vagabonds, but to have as much care of our modesty and chastity as if we had been at a school of virtue rather than a banquet."[79] Minucius Felix's writing in AD 210, entitled *Octavius*, revealed the atmosphere of criticism too by stating, "Our feasts are conducted not only with modesty but in sobriety; we do not prolong the conviva, the drinking party. But temper our gaiety with chaste conversation."[80] Again Cyprian, in his letter to Donatus, refers to using resounding psalms to temper the meal from any excess.[81] It is accurate to say that only eighty years after Christ instilled the vision of the dinner church, pressure was already mounting against its continuance.

An Average Night at Agape. There is ample evidence of an average evening at one of these dinner church gatherings, a service order of sorts. By the time of Ignatius in AD 115, the dinner church was setting a tone of thanksgiving and a joyful sound of glad and generous hearts praising God, unlike the gloom with which the later generations surrounded the Eucharist.[82] The joy of the Lord was pervasive in these fellowship meals. Also during that time, the Roman historian Pliny wrote to Emperor Trajan in AD 98–117 that these Christians were in the habit of meeting on a certain fixed day, singing a hymn to Christ, binding themselves not to commit wicked deeds; after which they partook of food, of an ordinary and innocent sort.[83] Pliny also reported that these first Christians were talkative, passionate, and sometimes quarrelsome as they met over evening meals to read Paul's letters.[84]

We get another glimpse of an average evening at a dinner church gathering in Tertullian's words from *Apologies* 39:16–19, which reads,

> Our dinner shows its idea in its name, Agape. Whatever the cost, with that refreshment we help the needy. Only so much is eaten as satisfies hunger. After water for the hands come the lights; and then each, from what he knows of the Holy Scriptures, or from his own heart, is called before the rest to prophesy. Prayer in like manner ends the banquet.[85]

We also have in Tertullian the term "Love Feast," and the emphasis on the feeding of the needy in this meal. He made it clear that it was a real banquet, a real meal, and a great setting for the Lord's Supper.[86] John Michael Perry wrote that prayers expressing the sacred meaning of the agape meals were always recited when they gathered.[87]

Those Who Attended. These dinner church gatherings were a mosaic of peoples; Christ-followers were present, to be sure, and so were the poor. "Chrysostom spoke of the church at Antioch. Though not wealthy, the church cared for three thousand widows and virgins daily, and cared for those in prison, sick and disabled, and those away from their homes. The church also provided food and clothing to those who came casually every day."[88] The dinner church demonstrated a significant concern for the poor. This seemed to grow in intensity through the centuries to the point that when Julian the Apostate became emperor after Constantine in AD 362, he instructed the pagan priests to imitate the Christians and their concern for hospitality and care for the poor and strangers. Hoping to reinstate paganism as the official religion of Rome, he complained, "These impious Galileans support not only their own poor but ours as well."[89]

So, a vibrant dinner church usually included the poor, but more were in attendance. Tertullian revealed that another standing invite was always in effect when he stated, "Men had to be attracted in from the existing if shallow fellowship of their pagan clubs and taverns by another fellowship which was richer and more rewarding."[90] Not only were the saved and the poor present; so were the pagans. The dinner church gathering was an interesting mosaic of people that consisted of the saved, the poor, the lonely, and pagans. Such was the atmosphere of the agape feasts. Then again, such was the atmosphere created by the Master himself when he walked the earth. No wonder the population of the redeemed grew in such profound ways.

Alan Hirsch noted that there were twenty-five thousand Christians by AD 100, but by AD 300, the population of Christians had swelled to twenty million believers. "Herein lies the powerful mystery of the Church."[91] I cannot help but note that this growth from thousands to millions occurred during the time when the dinner church vision was riding its highest wave.

The Demise of the Dinner Church

Asceticism. The first notions of decline for the dinner church appear in the Didache, which was drafted early in the second century, and it reflects the gradual disengagement of the Eucharist from the meal.[92] This was the first time a concern was revealed that the broken bread and cup should not come in contact with sinners. That created a problem for the dinner church because they regularly invited sinners to their dinners, and they regularly celebrated the bread and cup in the same evening. Though Tertullian continued to defend his agape meals, the bread and cup started to separate in some places during his time, AD 160–225, according to pastor and author Dan Kimball.[93] Within the next century, the criticism against the agape meals as being too joyful and conviva-like mounted to an official complaint. By the middle of the fourth century, an official debate developed in the Council of Laodicea (AD 363–364) that resulted in banning the agape meal as the rising tide of asceticism swept over the church and its theology.[94] The coup de grâce came in AD 692 at the Council of Trullian, where the dinner church was banned for life, never to return to the medieval church.[95]

Replacing Simplicity. Another problem that pressured the agape meals was that some hosts were using the meals to benefit themselves rather than practice the vision of Christ. In the fourth century, church leaders, such as Jerome, warned clergy who might be tempted to use hospitality to gain favor with the powerful instead of welcoming the poorest people to their tables. Jerome reminded them that if they once again welcomed the poor, they would have Christ as their guest.[96] Jerome's provocations did little to save the intent of the agape meal. The overwhelming idea regarding church during that period, as Constantine centralized Christianity as the state religion, was that worship needed to be reenvisioned with a new sense of scale. Simple ceremonies were replaced with elaborate performances, and house church simplicity yielded to imperial magnificence.[97] Witherington observed, "It did not augur well for the Lord's supper when the Church went mainstream and moved its meal out of the house and into the Church."[98] By the time we get to Clement of Hippolytus, we are a long way from what we find in Paul and the Gospels, where the influence of the Passover and the shared meal is still strongly present.[99] In this fateful fourth century, the church officially moved away from the framework of the Jewish meal and its graces to a purely Gentile milieu.[100] With that shift, the dinner church became a historical relic.

The Reformers' Choice. Though centuries later, the Reformation touches some edges of the agape meal's demise. Many aspects of original faith were recovered for the church in the early 1500s, but the dinner church vision was not one of them. Witherington stated that the reformers abandoned not only the meal context but the *koinonia* concept of discerning that we are the body of Christ.[101] "Although the reformers acknowledged that hospitality was a sacred act, they allowed no sacred space for it."[102] The Reformation was developing at the same time as modernity was coming. It was a time that emphasized cerebral faith, linear thinking, reason, and logical argument, and it was perceived that faith was arrived at by a mental acceptance of doctrines.[103] Against that backdrop, the vision of a dinner church did not make as much sense as sitting people in soldier rows and preaching the creeds in lecture form for an hour at a time. The educational format of spirituality was intentionally chosen over the experiential format of the agape meal. In that way the modern church remains more children of the reformers than children of the apostles.[104]

The Vision Resurfaces

The *Swiss Order*. There have been some brief resurgences of the agape meal church format in recent centuries, albeit in obscure locations. In 1527, a document called the *Swiss Order* emerged from Zollikon, Switzerland. The Reformation message splashed all over Europe, and different towns and groups developed their response to its new freedoms. Such was the case in Zollikon. However, unlike the other European townships, they decided to include the vision of the dinner church. "The *Swiss Order* Article 7 called for a commemorative meal," wrote author and professor Werner Packull. "When combined with the admonition of Article I, this would have meant a celebration of the Lord's Supper at least three or four times a week, presumably in conjunction with the common meal."[105] This was an actual resurgence of the agape meal. Again the age-old conflict arose, as some of these gatherings were mistakenly lumped in with other groups that encouraged debauchery and drunkenness, though the Zollikon agape meals did not do so. Nonetheless, the council of Zurich decided to suppress the first Anabaptist congregational experiment.[106]

The Moravians. That would not be the end of the effort, because when a small group of Christ-followers living in Marpeck's Circle, Moravia, got their hands on the *Swiss Order* and adapted it to fit their setting, the dinner church vision sprang to life again in Moravia.[107] For the Moravians, this was a very energetic event. They sang hymns, listened to music, talked to one another about their walk with Christ as they ate at the tables, and often ended the dinner with a lighted-candle ceremony. This was probably in remembrance of Tertullian's lamp-lighting habit preceding the spiritual discussions. Then a couple of years later, Jacob Hutter arrived to investigate what God was doing in Austerlitz, and saw a community of Christ-followers living as one heart, one mind, and one soul, each caring faithfully for the other.[108] He was moved by that vision of unity and started planting similar communities throughout the land. Between 1537 and 1545, many Hutterite communities sprang into existence.[109] These communities of approximately 150 people each entered into communal life together and, affected by a reading of the *Swiss Order*, many of them embraced the agape meal format.

Wesley's Famous Potlucks. Another resurgence of the agape meal occurred during Methodism and Wesley's famous potlucks. It was from those days that church potlucks were spoken of as an extension of the Eucharist, similar to the agape feasts of the early church.[110] Theologian James F. White noted that the agape meals were given a new lease on life by John Wesley.[111] Wesley prepared the attitudes of his followers to serve at his potluck feasts with statements such as "Whether they will finally be lost or saved, you are expressly commanded to feed the hungry, and clothe the naked."[112] Christine Pohl stated, "John Wesley deliberately employed early church models and recovered the practice of shared meals when he instituted love feasts."[113] Another thing Wesley envisioned was the blending of the poor and weak individuals with influential leaders, which was another significant return to early Christian understandings.[114] He further insisted on close, face-to-face relations among different kinds of people as they sat around his dinner tables.[115] In 1785, a group of Methodists, with the support of John Wesley, founded the Stranger's Friend Society in London, dedicated to ministry among the urban poor. They described the local poor as "strangers because of their 'sore affliction' and their inability to find relief . . . [they] had 'no helper' in society."[116] In so doing, Wesley took his shared table to England's central city. Thanks to John Wesley, the dinner church vision thrived again in the eighteenth century.

Contemporary Expressions

Interesting Portrayals. The twentieth century revealed a few more resurgences of the dinner church vision. Early on, the famed German pastor Dietrich Bonhoeffer stated, "The table fellowship of Christians implies obligation. We share our bread, thus we are firmly bound to one another. The one bread links us together. No one dares go hungry as long as another has bread."[117] While there is no historical evidence that Bonhoeffer's church ever engaged in an agape meal, his work as a theologian rightly captured the ancient attitude of the shared meal and has affected many Christians ever since. Also in Europe, early in the nineteenth century in Germany, England, and Holland, it is rumored that some groups shortened the agape meal to a representative celebration and served a sweetened bun, coffee, and sweetened milky tea, all dispensed in the pews by *dieners*, which is German for "servers." Some of these churches actually employed trombone choirs to walk through the streets, which was the call for everyone to come to the love feast. Some of the groups drafted back to the New Testament description of the Last Supper of Christ with the intent of reenacting it as closely as possible, including the foot washing as people would enter, just as

Jesus had done for his disciples. In America during that time, the Brethren Church practiced fellowship meals and served lamb or beef along with a bowl of soup.[118]

The Emerging Church. In this twenty-first century, an interesting variety of agape expressions is surfacing. Dan Kimball, pastor of Vintage Faith Church in Santa Cruz, California, observed, "Many emerging worship gatherings have a meal together before the actual formal gathering starts to further enhance their sense of community."[119] The emerging church and the house church movements find the agape meal to be a natural fit in many settings. Todd Johnson of Fuller Theological Seminary identified three basic kinds of churches in modern Western civilization: Word-organized churches, music-organized churches, and table-organized churches.[120] It is likely that Word-organized and music-organized churches will struggle to embrace an agape meal format, as those models are primarily stage-oriented; however, the table-organized churches have a very small leap to make from communion and reflective-based gatherings to a dinner church vision. The alignment of souls between the two is very close.

A Careful Lament

I offer this next section with a bit of uneasiness. The late Lesslie Newbigin, theologian and missionary to India, once wrote, "Criticizing one's own culture is like trying to push a bus while you are sitting in it."[121] I recognize that the comments that follow are being made from a questionable position, yet somehow a lament needs to be attempted regarding the ease with which the church has ignored the dinner vision.

Drops in the Bucket. While there have been bright spots on the dinner church landscape, such as the Moravians, the Hutterites, the Methodists, modern house churches, and emerging churches, they are only drops in the bucket. The truth is, hospitality and the Christian table disappeared as a significant moral practice in the

1700s. Socioeconomic changes steered hospitality toward benevolence organizations and government offices. The churches stepped away from any role associated with hospitality.[122] While the agape meal struggled for expression after the fourth century, the concept of hospitality remained a Christian duty, but by the end of the eighteenth century, it was emptied of its central moral meaning."[123]

Dilutions. Remnants of the original practices remain today, though most do not understand their origins. The offering, for instance, originated as the ancient practice of people bringing food for the feasts along with bread and wine for Communion. In time, the potlucks subsided and monetary gifts accompanied the bread and wine. After the gathering, the bread and money were taken out into the streets and shared with the poor. In modern days, money gifts have become the primary way to fund the buildings and programs of the church.[124] That dilution stands in contrast to the idea that most early Christians assumed that God had loaned property and resources so they could pass them on to those in need.[125] That attitude is ever so clear in the book of Acts, but for modern Christianity that attitude seems sparse. Instead of living to be Christ to the needy, we are living to create comfortable Christian worlds for ourselves. Harold Westing, an authority on church growth, made a brutal observation when he wrote that we are like the rich Corinthians who feasted without sharing their food with the poor. Modern Christians spend billions on new church construction every year. Would we go on building lavishly furnished, expensive church plants if members of our own congregations were starving?[126] That is where the conflict remains.

A Bridge Too Far. Avery Dulles, in his classic *Models of the Church*, stated, "The kerygmatic understanding of the church stands in tension with the institutional views."[127] The kerygmatic understanding is all about reaching out for the "least of these" (Matt. 25:40), while the modern institutional church is mostly about reaching those who are already like us. I do not think we have intended to become self-absorbed, but somehow we have ended up on these shores. C. S. Lewis uttered a similar lament not that many years ago: "It looks as if [the Anglican clergy] believe[s] people can be lured to go to church by incessant brightenings, lightenings, lengthenings, abridgements, simplifications, and complications of the service." The result is that "many give up churchgoing altogether" and the rest "merely endure."[128] Focusing on the comfort of the churchgoer has led us to an undesired and unproductive place. "Christianity has become a nice Sunday drive."[129] Ben Witherington summed up my lament well by saying, "We have come a long way from the Passover meal of AD 30, not just a bridge too far but many bridges too far."[130]

A Seattle Version

Food, Art, and Friendship. In 2009, Westminster Community Church decided to revisit the ancient fellowship meal. We started it with the thought that it might be a viable redemption plan, and we needed one. However, within a few short months of starting, it became a call, and then it became the central expression of our church. We now call ourselves Community Dinners, because our version of church is to host dinners each week in different neighborhoods for all who live there. The food is catered, a guitarist plays, an artist paints a picture that is inspired from a gospel story, and a couple hundred neighbors gather to eat and enjoy a warm meal with us in each of our sites every week. Church members mingle and eat amid our gathered neighbors. Friendships are quickly formed, and soon discussions turn into spiritual conversations.

Discussions about Christ. Near the beginning of the evening, one of the staff reads a short story from the Gospels and announces that a discussion about that reading will be held at the end for all who want to stay. Then, thirty minutes later, another staff member sits on a stool in the middle of the room and leads an open discussion. The conversation is usually very lively, and opinions about life, God, and spiritual things bounce around the room like an unmanned fire hose. The comments are often diverse, off-color, challenging, frequently hilarious, and always intriguing. Somehow, as the group is verbally processing a truth from Scripture, the Holy Spirit always seems to culminate the conversation into a spiritual and reflective moment. When that moment arrives, the staff leader leads in a prayer for the entire group that is directed to Christ and asks for strength to turn to him. We refer to this as a *prayer of turning*. The discussion and prayer seldom last longer than ten minutes. There is often such a feeling of favor in the room after the prayer that applause breaks out spontaneously.

Their Kind of Church. It never ceases to amaze us how many people intentionally wait after eating their meal for the Christ discussion and prayer; we are watching the vast majority of the attendees stay for the end at each of our sites. This is their church. Some time ago, I concluded that in twenty-nine years of ministry, I had not served in an environment where redemptive flow was naturally occurring. Now, because we revisited the agape meal and aligned ourselves to the dinner church vision, we know what redemptive flow feels like.

Summation

Something Has Shifted. Many assumptions about American life are imploding right now. One such assumption is that most people are living the American dream: everyone owns a house with a white picket fence. Suburbia errantly assumes that most people live as they do. The fact is that 60 percent of the US population now lives in multi-housing communities.[131] This suggests that people are thronging toward the urban cities. Kofi Annan, former secretary-general of the United Nations, stated that as of 2009, 50 percent of the world's population lived in the major cities.[132] Researcher Ed Stetzer noted that the effect of this population shift on Christ's kingdom is not small; the majority of these multi-housing dwellers will remain unreached unless churches are planted in these unique communities.[133] Our world is not what it used to be only twenty years ago, and our church world is not the same either. The time for a serious discourse about the dinner church vision is at hand. Author Charles

Trueheart, in describing "the next Church," predicted that it would have "no spires. No crosses. No robes. No clerical collars. No hard pews. No kneelers. No biblical gobbledygook. No prayer rote. Nor fire. Nor brimstone. No pipe organs. No dreary eighteenth-century hymns. No forced solemnity. No Sunday finery. No collection plates."[134] If Trueheart's vision of the future is right, many things about the American church are scheduled for demolition. In a day like this, if we are able to consider and embrace some of the ancient ideas that marked the first church, we might find a great new ministry awaiting us. George Barna observed, "Perhaps as much as anything else, the church is better poised than any other institution in America to respond to the rampant loneliness of the American people."[135] That is no small open door in society. When the societal call of poverty joins voices with the societal call of loneliness, the church has a very real invite back to prominence in some very sore spots in our American culture. Hearing those twin voices sets the stage for seeing the dinner church vision again.

A Church-Planting Model. The American church finds itself in a situation where we need to seriously increase our church-planting efforts, especially in the large cities. Almost every denomination in America is feeling this urgency and working toward that end. As encouraging as this is, the actual church-planting rate is not commensurate with all of the talk. Accordingly, there is no small call being sounded for the American church to step up its actual church-planting pace. I would propose to any church-planting team that they consider the dinner church vision among the other options. The attraction models and the incarnational models are not the only two choices; the dinner church model is a very real option that has theological richness and might be the best choice in sore neighborhoods and in the hands of certain teams.

Connect the Spheres. An agape meal creates several societal bridges. Initially, it connects the spheres between the home and the public (*oikis* and *polis*) and gives people who have fallen through the cracks of society a family. One lady, who had been orphaned as a thirteen-year-old remarked, "It's not just about food, you know, it's about knowing someone cares."[136] An agape meal also connects the spheres between the natural world and the supernatural one, similar to what Abraham, Gideon, Israel's leaders, and the two men on the road to Emmaus experienced, when our Lord takes a seat beside us, and miraculous and unexplainable things happen.

An agape meal connects the spheres between Christians and the Great Commission by giving them a place to express the behaviors of Christ. There are many places to express the character of Christ, but few places actually engage in the ministry behaviors of Christ, such as healing, serving, touching, caring, embracing, offering comfort, breathing courage, and inspiring faith. Christine Pohl, speaking of her own experience, stated, "I discovered just how heavy large pots of soup could be and just how precious it was to share a meal with a lonely person."[137] There are thousands and thousands of American Christians who are in need of that same precious discovery.

Finally, an agape meal connects the spheres between the beginning and the end; God's first words to Adam surrounded eating, and some of God's final words in Revelation surround the warm welcome to his great feast. Every time we eat an agape meal, we are experiencing yet another divine stepping-stone between God's first and last message for humanity—he wants to be with us and have supper with us. Listen to his heartfelt invitation again:

> "Look! I stand at the door and knock. If you hear my voice and open the door, I will come in, and we will share a meal together as friends." (Rev. 3:20)

God uses the metaphor of food and dinner too many times for us to ignore. Could it be that our Lord chose the dinner church vision with an eternal message in mind? That group of Christians in Bithynia in AD 112, who met to sing hymns to Christ and share a common meal, were our spiritual ancestors, and they offer an attractive picture to us today.[138] Perhaps the dinner church vision will fan into a flame again.

A LOCALIZED APOSTOLIC MIND-SET

Recapturing Sent-ness and Citywide-ness

The apostolic era was a profound season, both spiritually and sociologically. Alan Hirsch, founding director of the Forge Mission Training Network, stated that those initial efforts signified the powerful mystery of the church, as it grew from twenty-five thousand to twenty million in just two hundred years.[1] This world has never before or since seen such a per capita movement as the original spread of Christianity. Today, the notable expansions of Christianity are occurring south of the equator, but the Northern Hemisphere is suffering significant declines. "In 1900, Europe and North America comprised 82 percent of the world's Christian population. In 2005, it comprises 39 percent."[2] The last one hundred years have witnessed a significant shift of Christian influence from the North to the South. There is a need to recapture the powerful mystery of the apostolic era in the West.

I am concerned that many Christian leaders have forgotten what it feels like to hold an apostolic mind-set. Hirsch believes that the apostolic genius that drove the first church was a constellation of six elements that included the lordship of Jesus at its heart, the missional-incarnational impulse, disciple making, a sense of comradeship and community, organic systems, and an apostolic environment.[3] Apostolic thinking can no longer be reserved for foreign missions or church planting: an all-hands-on-deck response is needed from the body of Christ if we are to restore a healthy apostolicism—healthy enough to reengage our cities.

The Apostolic Era

What began as a powerful movement that literally reconfigured the dominant social landscape of its day, ultimately lost its fervor. The apostolic era gave way to the Christendom era, which, in turn, had to make way for the Reformation era. (The latter two still exist in various forms to this day.[4]) The Reformation church is primarily a proclamation-based church; the Christendom church is primarily a sacred-space church; and the apostolic church was primarily a dinner church, but with the Edict of Milan in

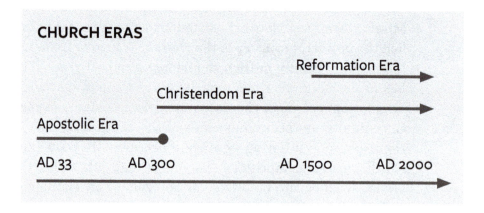

AD 313, the age of the missional-apostolic church came to an end. Constantine moved Christianity from a marginalized, subversive, and persecuted movement to the favored religion of the state; everything changed.[5] From that fateful day until the present, the church has been confused by competing messages. E. V. Hill once said, "The gospel says, 'Go' but our church buildings say, 'Stay.' The gospel says, 'Seek the lost,' but our churches say, 'Let the lost seek the church.'"[6]

Not long after the Edict of Milan, the post-apostolic church developed a closed Communion in which those who were not baptized were excluded from the table. That was markedly different from the apostle Paul's theology; he never excluded people from the table on the basis of their sinfulness.[7] Yet, by the end of the fourth century, a theological impediment stood firmly between the sinner and the Savior. The church has labored under the burden of patrolling the border between the saved and the unsaved ever since. That is something the early apostles did not dwell on; they were simply too busy pouring out the good news on one and all.

During the Reformation of the sixteenth century, several things were set right, but restoring an apostolic mind-set was not one of them. Ed Stetzer wrote, "Geography caused the Reformation Church to look inward. Polemics against Catholicism forced it away from the apostolic nature of the Church."[8] The simple fact is, the Reformation occurred during a time when Europe was almost completely Christianized.[9] Thus, a strong apostolic missiology was not needed. However, in this day, we find ourselves in a completely different missiological situation, and yet we are still using the proclamation-based church model of the reformers. Former president of Mattersay Hall, UK, Paul Alexander worded it this way: "We are more sons of the reformers than sons of the apostles."[10]

It is interesting to note that the definition of "heresy" comes from *hairesus*, which means "choosing for oneself over against the apostolic tradition."[11] Yet, church history reveals one step followed by another, leading away from the apostolic mind-set of "sent-ness" and "city-wideness" to the point that in this day we can barely comprehend what apostolic urgency looks like.

Apostolicism Relegated to Foreign Missions and Church Planting

It appears that most evangelical churches only express their apostolic urge by supporting a missionary or a church planter. While anything that advances the gospel is worthy of accommodation, it is not the same as the apostolic thinking that pulsated in those first centuries. Many denominations can be very proud of their foreign missions efforts and the apostolic mind-set that has guided us; however, we live in a day when our home churches are stalling. The same apostolic urge that drove us to the ends of the earth now needs to drive us into our own neighborhoods. That is America's great challenge, and it requires more than a casual and financial engagement with missionaries and church planters.

Church planting in America is in need of significant critique. While almost every denomination in America has church-planting plans on their books, the historical fact remains that the church-planting rate in America is as low as it was during the Civil War and the Great Depression.[12] According to church pollster David Olson, the American church would need to triple their church-planting rate just to stay on par with the population growth in America, as it has grown by 91,384,566 since 1990.[13] Our church-planting plans are woefully behind the need. A version of an apostolic urge that

Churches Started per 1 Million Residents
Based on Start Dates of 92,677 Churches in the United States

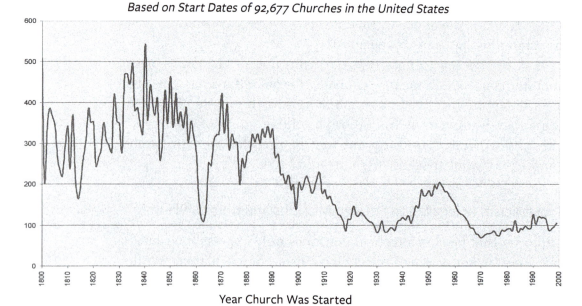

Year Church Was Started

© 2004 by David T. Olson

is beyond throwing a few dollars at church planters must arrive on our shores if we are going to recover the church-to-population ratios we held only twenty years ago. The American church desperately needs to step up its church-planting pace.

A second critique of American church planting is associated with where we are locating our precious few plants. American church planting in its present form is not as apostolic as most assume. According to Alan Hirsch, "Church planting has generally been restricted to areas where churches are already flourishing, leaving many underprivileged areas untouched."[14]

Ed Stetzer observed, "More and more church planters seem to target the upwardly mobile middle-class suburbanite. It appears that God has had a special burden for places with hundreds of new homes compared to the inner city with thousands of old homes."[15] The very nature of apostolic function is to identify social circles where the good news is being underserved and find a way to turn on the light of Christ to those people, yet there is now a value system that directs church planters to go only where they know they can grow a church and to places where they want to raise their families. While this has produced fruit, it is something different from the apostolic mind-set. New Testament scholar Douglas Moo interpreted Paul's writings to the Christians in Rome as a charge against them: "They could not be classified as an actual church because they evidenced no apostolic urge; that they lacked the apostolic imprimatur that was necessary to constitute a church; that they needed to rehearse the fundamental kerygma that would turn a Christian community into a Christian church."[16] Paul was giving the Christians in Rome the opportunity they needed to gain actual church status by joining his apostolic plans. This is an important demarcation; it is possible to be a Christian community but not a Christian church. The genuine Christian church of Jesus Christ has a strong and continual apostolic urge that forces it outward. An apostolic imprimatur, or apostolic urge, is very different from extending the church to a place where a planter wants to raise a family. Rather, it advances into locations where the gospel is least present.

The founders of the Pentecostal movement originally thought in apostolic terms. The published goal by some denominations in those early days was that there be one church per twenty-five thousand Americans.[17] Church planters were naturally focused on the places where that ratio was not represented. Today that apostolic thinking has become diluted to include any new church plant in any US location just because a planter wants to go there. It appears that the punchy, Paul-like, apostolic version of church expansion is all but lost on us. This has translated into atrocious ratios in our urban centers of one church to 101,000 people in our US cities; our apostolic urge has slipped away. Were Paul here today, he would likely call us out as he did the Roman believers and question our church status as he questioned theirs. For our cities to again become targeted by church planters, a renewed apostolic imprimatur must arise in all of our leadership conversations. We cannot ignore our cities and then consider ourselves adept missiologists in our own land.

Silo-Ism

Apostolic expansion creates a problem for those who are deeply mired in proclamation-based thinking. Ed Stetzer noted that parish mentality is the primary reason the church-to-population ratio is declining, because new churches are not started in new areas because they would be too close to other established churches of the same denomination.[18] This form of silo-ism seems to flow naturally from congregational-based values, which instinctively protect its potential attenders. This stands in contrast with the apostolic mind-set, which identifies and targets unreached social circles that might only be blocks away from present churches, but who are unable to speak the language of that tribe. No group can reach every social circle in their sphere, but it requires maturity on the part of a proclamation-based church to admit that. Alan Hirsch referred to the transition from one fundamental form of church to another as "liminality," and such a shift necessitates the apostolic role.[19] In other words, a group will feel lost for a season while they navigate from congregation-centric thinking to apostolic-centric thinking. It takes boldness for a church to make this transition, but some churches do possess the courage to leave silo-ism behind.

There is another form of silo-ism to be considered. Suburban churches that are serving middle- and upper-income populations feel little responsibility to spread the gospel to nearby neighborhoods with lower-income populations. This is a case where leaders have drawn the lines of their obligation in ways that are comfortable for them, but not so comfortable for their struggling neighbors. Ideas such as "the indigenous church" and "sovereignty of church" actually have a dark side; they give leaders the right to ignore the apostolic concept of "the church of a city" that we see in the New Testament. These forms of silo-ism undermine apostolic efforts. Rick Rusaw of LifeBridge Christian Church (Longmont, Colorado) suggested that the great challenge of ministry to sore neighborhoods is that leaders who are most in touch with the needs of the challenged people often have the least ability and capacity to meet those needs.[20] How frustrating it is for church planters to know how to apostolically spread into lower-income neighborhoods but lack the resources to do so. A suburban congregation feeling entitled to pay for its own dreams while ignoring its nearby sore neighborhoods lacks an apostolic imprimatur; embracing the New Testament idea of "the church of a city" might cause leaders to build simpler buildings so they can have more resources to spread into challenged locations.

There is a movement in the church world to find new relevance in this day; however, placing new shifts back into proclamation-based ecclesiologies reduces the efforts to simple wordplay. Merely changing leadership terminology from traditional church language to apostolic and missional language while still rooted in church-growth theory with highly gifted CEO-type leaders does little to address the malaise of the church in the West.[21] Much of the present missional movement is caught up in this muted pursuit of relevance. Alan Johnson stated that the term "missional" has now achieved buzzword status and is often used for anything that reinvents church to make it more attractive to people."[22] This does not lead to the same thing that an apostolic mind-set does. The redemption mission is not an equal initiative among other initiatives in the church; somehow it must be given singular priority status. Presbyterian missiologist Darrell Guder admitted, "It has taken us decades to realize that mission is not just a program of the church . . . it defines the church as God's sent people."[23] Adopting an apostolic mind-set prioritizes the redemption mission as the first mission.

The American church stands at a critical crossroads. The problem for the church of the West is that the world changed but the operational mode of the church has not.[24] To stay the course means to continue with the proclamation-based approaches that have been functioning for five hundred years. The other option is to consider a turn onto an apostolic-centric path. The declines in our churches are pervasive enough to warrant significant consideration at this juncture. Darrell Guder stated, "The church confronts the challenge of disengaging itself from the privileges of a previous church culture."[25] It is time to consider the radical option of reducing our obsession with proclamation-based approaches and the silo-isms they incubate, and instead lean into apostolic mind-sets that can pour the favor of Christ into our own streets and neighborhoods.

The Empty Chair

The apostle played a splendid role on the leadership team of the first church. What a different structure the church would have been without the apostles fulfilling their role of expanding the borders! The need for apostles in that day is the same need we have in this day. How else could one interpret Ephesians 4:11: "Now these are the gifts Christ gave to the church: the apostles, the prophets, the evangelists, and the pastors and teachers." This specific list of giftings for the church must have been important because the previous three verses reveal that releasing these gifts was the first thing Jesus did upon his ascension. To ignore any one of these gifts would be to change the intent of Christ and the outcome upon the life of his church. Also, the order of these stated gifts is an important consideration; the apostolic gift creates an environment for the prophetic, which creates an environment for the evangelistic, which creates an environment for the pastoral, which creates an environment for teaching.[26] To remove the apostle's voice from any leadership team is akin to removing the quarterback from a football team. Not much happens on the field without the quarterback putting the ball in motion; not much happens in the church without the apostle putting the gospel in motion. Alan Hirsch lamented, "We bemoan the current preference in churches for pastors and teachers at the exclusion of apostles, prophets, and evangelists."[27] It appears that the pastoral and teaching types have ejected the apostles, prophets, and evangelists from the system.[28] This is especially true in the church-growth model that swept into the American church in the 1970s. It is likely that the apostolic urge has been missing for long enough that we barely remember what it looks like. The apostolic mind-set identifies and enters the dark places of our cities, and this expansive thinking propels the rest of the leaders and the churches they serve into a new place and expression. Apostolic leaders create fields for the body of Christ that result in a gospel harvest, much the way a farmer plants a field in which a harvest will soon be emerging.[29] The simple fact is this: it is the apostles who create redemptive ministry for the rest of the church. "The evangel must be made known. The good news is to be shared. Disciples are to become apostles."[30] If the church ever needed its apostle-people to arise and focus their function on our local cities, it is now.

Restoring the Apostolic Urge

The apostolic urge is a punchy thing. Noel Tichy, the management guru, referred to the apostolic spirit as emotional, energetic, and edgy. Pastor Bill Hybels called it "holy discontent."[31] The circuit riders of the American West and the Chinese church were examples of rugged apostolic leadership, riding out to small towns, establishing churches, and then moving on to other under-gospeled areas.[32] There are church movements in this day that have reduced Jesus to a witty rabbi, a superstar, and a wandering charismatic, but they lack the persuasive power that the original apostles served up.[33] However, this edgy apostolic urge is not a stranger to Pentecostal history. Daniel Tomberlin of the Church of God (Cleveland, Tennessee) tells us that "Pentecostals understood the outpouring of the Holy Spirit to be the 'latter rain,' that is the restoration of apostolic Pentecost upon the last-days church."[34] Pentecostals understand apostolic urgency; it is deeply embedded in our history.

Apostles have a unique way of looking at their communities; they can stand beside the other leadership gifts and see open doors for the gospel that pastors and teachers miss. Alan Hirsch contended that "apostolic insight and genius is coded into each community through latent DNA, only most of us cannot see it."[35] The early apostles came to terms with the notion that they had to do what only they could do.[36] Apostles have an internal lens that others simply do not have—an internal compass that gives direction.[37] When the apostolic urge rises in a church, that church starts to see darkened social circles in neighborhoods near them, and for some indefinable reason they know what to do about it. That is apostolic genius at work.

The Holy Struggle

The apostolic path is not as easy as the congregation-comforted path. "The ministry of the apostles was marked by opposition, persecution, and suffering."[38] The passages of Scripture and the following church history that chronicled the apostolic era make it clear that this road is not for the faint of heart; courage and boldness are required. However, there is divine purpose in the pain. In fact, it is a necessary holy struggle. Apostolic paths require greater dependency upon divine power. Dependency must be practiced and learned; leaders and churches learn that dependency only one way—through holy struggle. Persecution drove the early Christian movements and the Chinese church to discover their truest nature as an apostolic people.[39] A people that are forced into measures of sacrifice learn to lean into God's redemptive plans and learn to lean into their apostolic calling. The holy struggle takes people from knowing what to live for to knowing what to sacrifice for. Knowing what to struggle for is no small spiritual achievement. The apostolic path is not for trendy church planters as much as for those who are able to embody the age-old poem:

> We the willing, led by the unknowing, are doing the impossible for the incapable. We have done so much with so little for so long that we are now qualified to do anything with nothing.
>
> —Anonymous

A Functional Apostolicism

We live in a day where we are fourteen hundred years removed from the most generous placement of the conclusion of the apostolic era. While we can observe the values of the apostles by studying the New Testament, developing a functional and local apostolicism is quite another matter. It requires focus. Alan Johnson wrote, "An apostle is focused on gospelizing; it carries the sense of being very narrow and focused."[40] The field of leadership has become such a complex set of principles that it overwhelms the simple apostolic mind-set. In contrast, apostolic function means there are some things that we choose not to do.[41]

A functioning apostle translates the good news for a social circle in ways that neighborhoods will value. The first apostles had no problem changing their explanations of the gospel to speak to a different social circle. "Jesus' phrase 'kingdom of God or heaven' in the Gentile milieu was not particularly helpful or meaningful. The apostles found it inconvenient. Accordingly we hear less and less about 'kingdom of God' and an increase of synonyms like 'salvation.'"[42] We expect our foreign missionaries to translate the gospel both verbally and culturally; local apostles must now function the same way—even in America.

The American church primarily assumes they are there to serve good, middle-class people. The apostolic mind-set assumes some different starting points. The Acts church planted churches with apostolic DNA with an apostolic theology that held a deep concern for the marginalized and physically impoverished people.[43] Similarly, today's functioning apostles look for local "social lift" entry points in their cities. Alan Johnson argued that "evangelism without social action is not holistic mission."[44] The local apostles count it an honor to first serve the gospel before proclaiming the gospel; however, many Christian leaders do not share their enthusiasm for social engagement and question whether that approach is doing the "real work" of the gospel. "Expressions of Christian social concern can end up being a kind of unwanted stepchild that is viewed as eating up precious resources, and the fear that evangelism will be eroded by the press of caring for physical needs."[45] It is interesting how Christian leaders can so easily draw a line between serving the gospel and speaking it. Missiologist Ralph Winters observed, "In the case of a family member, you would never think about choosing between evangelism and social action. Relationship provides the context for interpretation."[46]

Somehow, the American church has moved social engagement to the back burner, and in so doing has blocked a primary door for apostolic entry into new social circles and new neighborhoods. There are only three major missions perspectives alive today: church growth, unreached peoples, and social concern.[47] The American church would do well to consider the social concern doors that exist in their cities, especially if the church-growth door is not opening well for them.

A functioning apostle preaches a very different way to a very different crowd. To teach scriptural insight to a Sunday morning crowd is not the same thing as preaching to an unreached social circle, and yet we broad-brush our messages across everyone with the assumption that we are doing the gospel work. We are not. "Standing in stark contrast to apologetic theology is kerygmatic theology, whose adherents place their trust in the apostolic proclamation or kerygma, rather than in apologetic strategies."[48] In this day when apologetics, exegetics, word studies, and hermeneutics fill the tool kit of the speaker, we feel we do a disservice if we do not use them all. While that might make for excellent teaching, it is not apostolic preaching. Preaching (the kerygma) is the retelling of the simple stories of Christ.

Early in the second century, Papias informed us that Mark was not an eyewitness of Christ, but was the interpreter of Peter and wrote down what he remembered of Peter's preaching.[49] The gospel of Mark is the best example of apostolic and kerygmatic preaching, and yet is the simplest of the books in the Bible; it is merely a recitation of the parables and stories surrounding the life of Christ. The apostles saw preaching as throwing the stories of Christ into the lives of the hearers as if they were a stone.[50]

A functional apostolicism knows the difference between Christian teaching and kerygmatic preaching. Merold Westphal wrote, "The first-order Christian discourse: it is kerygma, not apologetics."[51] Teaching and exegetical tools are good for the "already saved" on Sunday morning, but preaching the simple stories of Jesus is the apostle's manner of speaking because of the way it invites the lost into the life of Christ.

Sent-ness

The term *apostle* is used eighty times in the New Testament, and refers to "one sent forth on a special mission."[52] Professor of pastoral theology Robert Anderson believes that "apostle" and "missionary" are identical in meaning—one who is sent forth.[53] Yet even with the abundance of "sent" Scriptures and "sent" roles, Western Christianity has lost the theology and practice of "sent-ness" on the home front. Alan Johnson noted that the statistics demonstrate that we are following a missiology that says missionaries are most needed not where non-Christians are, but where Christians are.[54] The classical doctrine of *missio Dei*, which is God the Father sending the Son and the Son sending the Spirit, is now expanded to include the Father, Son, and Holy Spirit sending the church to the world.[55] Karl Barth first proposed the idea of "God's sending" to the Brandenburg Missionary Conference in 1932, which contributed to the formation of missional theology and the *missio Dei*.[56] The *missio Dei* (sent-ness) is not just a recent concept; the New Testament model of church was conceived as a call to join a body of people who are sent on a mission.[57]

There are corners where the church is being reconceived as a people, brought together by a common calling to be a sent people.[58] This renewal is being forced into place by the growing number of proclamation-centric churches that are stalled, shrinking, and closing. Crossing cultural boundaries by crossing a geographic boundary was the iconic understanding of the occupation of the missionary, and is now a mandate for the churches to do the same in the West.[59] To enter new social circles in our own cities will require churches to renew the theology and practice of sent-ness. The churches of America must learn to do the complex work of rooting the gospel in nearby social circles in such a way that the good news actually sounds like good news to the people who live there.[60] Even the Archbishops of Canterbury's Commission on the Urban Priority Areas (ACUPA) is recommending lessening seminary instruction toward pastoral care of existing congregations, and increasing instruction oriented toward the missionary calling.[61] Mission theology is on the rise; the practice of sent-ness is rebounding.

Restoring apostolic sent-ness means we are going to have to adopt a missionary stance, a sending approach rather than an attractional one, and adopt best practices in cross-cultural missionary methodology for our local ministries.[62] Proclamation-based approaches cannot enter many social circles that make up the newly tribalized America. This is not merely a cultural statement, but also a physical one. Churches on average need one acre for every 150 people; that is hard to come by in Manhattan, where it costs millions per acre to exist.[63] "If evangelicals are to be successful in reaching North American urban centers, we must abandon the thinking that ten acres of land and a brick building are essential to be successful."[64] Ed Stetzer said, "The Singapore solution gives direction to North American urban areas, as they meet in hotels and office buildings."[65] Sent-ness into neighborhoods becomes conceivable if we are not assuming land and space and brick and mortar. Space issues are nonissues to a group with an unleashed apostolic mind-set. "Cosmic in vision, alive in praxis, apostolic in spirit, Pentecostal by nature, the church thrives where its mission theology flourishes freely."[66]

Citywide-ness

The apostolic mind-set is a citywide mind-set. The American church has been far more effective at placing our apostolic thinkers on the foreign fields than in our big cities, and yet it is the urban centers where the population is swelling. Tom Sine, founder of Mustard Seed Associates, reported that we are now an urban planet with more than 50 percent of the population living in large cities, and that the urban population will increase to 60 percent by 2020.[67] In the United States the urban population rose from 22 million to 113 million from 1890 to 1960.[68] America, too, is an urban nation. However, we are not adjusting to that fact very well. According to James K. A. Smith, author and editor of *Comment* magazine, "One of modernity's most insidious practices involves a flight from the messy realities of urban community."[69] The American church seems to be following the cues of American society and adopting distancing attitudes from urban challenges. The population is pouring into the exact places the American church is speedily vacating. That is not an apostolic value. One of George Barna's recommendations for the church in the year 2000 was this:

> As the turn of the century approaches, the wisest strategy would be to locate congregations in areas where the population is moving and growing. It means establishing strong urban ministries, not just providing a local presence in suburbs, establishing new and vibrant churches within our cities and addressing peculiar needs of city dwellers.[70]

Here we are, almost a quarter century down the road from 2000, and it does not appear that our attitudes toward our cities have shown any movement.

While the average church leader may not desire to pour his or her life into locations with urban-like issues, the apostolic leader is gritty and gutsy and welcomes the challenges. Evangelist Michael Green noted,

> The strategy nor the tactics of the first Christians were particularly remarkable. What was remarkable was their conviction, their passion, and their determination to act as Christ's embassy to a rebel world. They did most of their evangelism on what we would call secular ground. You find them in the laundries, at the street corners, and in the wine bars talking about Jesus to all who would listen. This was especially true in the urban insulae, where people lived in close proximity to one another in small apartments.[71]

The big cities have held significant opportunities for the gospel over the ages. Urban centers are not places to be avoided; they are places where great chapters of Christian history have been written. The success of the gospel in urban centers dates back to the book of Acts: "you have filled all Jerusalem with your teaching about him" (Acts 5:28). Then in the big Hellenistic cities in the Pax Romana that Paul strategically sought and through the time of Tertullian, the gospel spread so thoroughly that the term *pagan* (which originally meant "country-dweller") came to mean all who lived outside the major cities, those unlikely to have been exposed to the Christian faith.[72] Next, the famous Constantinian chapter of the fourth century established the Church of Rome and spread it from city to city throughout the world. The Reformation churches, too, found their way into the big cities of Germany and the Western world. During the days of the Great Awakening, the gospel again touched the big cities of England and Europe. In the nineteenth century, Salvation Army workers deliberately took on a liminal identity so they could become friends with the urban poor.[73] "In 19th century America, devout Christians developed inner-city missions to help ease newcomers' adjustments to urban life and rescued its castoffs."[74]

The Pentecostal revival in America began in the early 1900s at the Azusa Street Mission in Los Angeles, where Christians had gathered to collectively respond to the poverty in the streets. From that urban experience, several Pentecostal denominations were born. It is interesting how Pentecostal theology seems to ignore the implications of the urban setting when retelling the Pentecostal story. And yet, that is an important backdrop of our story: God obviously responding to our forefathers as they were responding to the urban poor in a citywide effort. Quite literally, some Pentecostal denominations were born on the streets among the poor. Through the ages, church history is filled with examples of how urban cities and sore neighborhoods are native territory for the gospel. The apostolic mind-set thrives in cities and cherishes the opportunity to pursue citywide redemption plans.

Apostolic leaders look at cities and see open doors in the exact places where other leaders see barriers. Many churches that reside in cities lack the apostolicism to see the open doors all around them. Missiology professor Kathyrn Mowry stated, "It seems a trend for urban congregations that the mission becomes social involvement while the church remains limited to a fellowship of urban missionaries. They reach out through many costly programs, but have not allowed the stranger to be one of them."[75] Even while offering a helping hand, one can remain insulated from the people who are not socially similar. For churches to embrace their opportunities, they need a theology and a sociology that enables a permeable border. Alan Johnson maintained that,

> more current views of sociocultural theory help us see that bounded groups are complex, that people often participate in many groups, that human personality resists closure, that anthropology has moved beyond functionalism to see diffusion, acculturation, permeability of cultural boundaries, migration, urbanization, and material conditions.[76]

In other words, city people are more ready to embrace different people, even Christ-people, than most churches are. City church leaders must cease the practice of gathering birds of a feather and instead consider prisoners, taxi drivers, and drug addicts to be worthy targets of the gospel, similar to the work of a missionary seeking a linguistic group.[77] Once the church is affected by the apostolic mind-set, the city becomes a sea of opportunity. Functioning in urban settings among diverse peoples is native territory for the church. Johnson called these ministries "urban conglomerate churches" because of the way they weld such diverse peoples together around Christ.[78] The urban church does not gain respect in their city with the safety of sameness; it gains respect from embracing the chaos of diverse peoples. Where most leaders see borders, apostolic leaders see another door into another social circle and another entry into another neighborhood.

Another trait of citywide-ness is that apostles notice the same kinds of groups that Christ noticed—the sore spots of society. Sore-spot targeting is our Christian heritage. In urban cities this has special meaning because there are so many broken people who live there. "The postmodern church must be willing to embrace, above all, those who have been crushed by the underside of modernity that inhabit the urban core of our cities."[79] One such sore spot is isolation and loneliness. Nearly half of our country's population are single; this social phenomenon is especially noticed in the urban centers.[80] This is a significant open door for the gospel for any apostolic group that is willing to include and befriend the stranger. This is the thinking behind "third place" social efforts. A person lives in his or her first place, works in his or her second place, but without a third place, urban areas fail to nourish relationships and diverse human contact that are the essence of the city.[81] Third place creation is more than space design; it must actually bond isolated people to a social circle. The church, with our rich history in fellowship and brotherhood, can be great at creating third places for the lonely.

The most significant sore spot in any city is the poor. Surprising percentages of the urban population live beneath the poverty line.

However, it seems that those whom Christ sought first are being sought last by his church. The gospel and food have been served together since the days of Christ. Even in later years, when the full Communion meal was reduced to bread and wine, there was still a deep connection to the marginalized. According to Professor Leanne Van Dyk of Western Theological Seminary, the Communion services in earlier centuries ended with Christians taking the left-over Communion bread out to the poor following the gathering.[82]

Seeking to lift the poor is perhaps the quickest way for a church to gain influence in their city, even among the upper classes; however, it is not without special challenges. "Starting a church among the urban poor will have different cost factors than planting among the urban elite."[83] Accordingly, part of the apostolic function is to lean on the divine Provider to provide bread from many sources, financial partners, funding streams, and tithing Christians with which to lift the poor that they are called to serve. Soong-Chan Rah, an associate professor of church growth and evangelism at Chicago's North Park Theological Seminary, observed that "the church-growth edge for urban centers is not affluent white churches, but poor disenfranchised immigrant churches."[84] Urban cities are filled with complex problems, but for the apostolic leader with citywide-ness coursing through his or her veins, it is the highest honor to bring the resources of God to the broken people on their streets.

The apostolic mind-set has been crafted by God to affect cities— whole cities. "It is God who makes apostles and grants the gift mixes to be able to bring the intangible atmosphere and the matrix of apostolicity that leads to the emergence of missional churches."[85] Ralph Winters believes that "missions in contrast to evangelistic organizations are in the lock-picking business. They are the ones whose unique skill is pioneering, getting inside of a culture that is bafflingly strange."[86] Our urban centers, above all other locations in our nation, are in desperate need of the apostles of the church to arise, to behold their city, to see the open doors, to pick the missional lock, and to make bold plans to serve the good news from neighborhood to neighborhood until the whole city feels the favor of the gospel. That is citywide-ness.

Summation

The American church has been dominated by pastors and teachers long enough. While we are wiser and better nurtured because of their ministries, we now find ourselves in desperate need of a functional apostolic mind-set—one that propels us into our own neighborhoods with a vibrant vision for the unreached social circles that live within the shadows of our buildings. The apostolic values of sent-ness and citywide-ness are big ideas, ideas big enough to overwhelm any inward thinking and create churches with mission in their hearts and practical redemption plans in their hands.

ORGANIC APPROACHES

Evaluating the Sociological Constructs of Churches

Most serious students of modern culture sense that tremendous change is afoot in our world and in the church. According to Peter Drucker, clearly the top management thinker of his day, "Every few hundred years throughout Western history, a sharp transformation has occurred where society altogether rearranges itself, its worldview, its basic values, its social and political structures, its arts, its key institutions. Fifty years later a new world exists."[1] It is not just the world that is rearranging itself; the church is feeling the need to rearrange itself too.

In this shifting season, most congregation-based churches that have enjoyed decades of success are now losing their ability to influence their communities. Reggie McNeal, missional leadership specialist for Leadership Network of Dallas, claimed that the Westernized Constantinian order is collapsing and the organic church is taking root.[2] Many new church plants and even some existing congregation-based churches need to consider organic constructs, especially in the cities. Alton Garrison contended that "we must seep into the cracks and crevices of our society with our Christ-like presence, our Christ-like thinking, our Christ-like behavior."[3] But this is exactly the problem; thousands of Christ-families have lost their ability to seep into their culture.

To add urgency to frustration, said Dallas Theological Seminary's Aubrey Malphurs, smaller churches are presently in deep decline and are truly in trouble; they may not have even three years for making critical changes.[4] New manners of seeping into our neighborhoods are not only needed; they are needed quickly. Understanding organic constructs might offer some hope for church planters and existing church leaders. After all, "seeping" is easy for organic churches.

Organic Sociology

Few leaders question the sociological makeup of their churches; they just accept the Reformation church template as an enduring assumption. The ones that are questioning it are the younger church planters. However, when they try to explain their organic vision, they are met with resistance from an older ministerial generation who jump to the conclusion that organic means "unorganized." A good description of an organic sociology is needed; even the younger leaders need help to better explain their vision.

Several authors have articulated the values of organic constructs. In the past few years, Neil Cole wrote *Organic Church*;[5] Thom Rainer and Eric Geiger wrote *Simple Church*;[6] and Dave Ferguson, Jon Ferguson, and Eric Bramlett wrote *The Big Idea*.[7] All of these missives cast an organic vision for church leaders. While each of these authors has made valuable contributions to the organic conversations, the one who gives the best definition is Soong-Chan Rah in his book *The Next Evangelicalism*, in which he reveals the sociological uniqueness of an organic construct. Rah wrote, "Primary cultures and secondary cultures yield two very distinct value systems. Primary is personal with a focus on people and relationships with an extended sense of nuclear family; secondary is systems and machines with a focus on objects and knowledge with a post-nuclear family."[8] All social structures are constructed in such a way that the needs of the persons involved are met. In primary social circles, the needs of the participants are met by a small core of people at the center in familial fashion—like a family unit or a mom-and-pop store. In secondary social circles, participants' needs are met by a set of systems that have been developed by the organization, such as businesses or larger churches. The secondary culture is a system-based culture; the primary culture is an organic culture. When younger leaders are talking about being more organic, what they are attempting to say is that they feel a call to be less systems-dependent and more relational-centric in the way ministry is dispensed. There is certainly nothing wrong with that initiative. Primary social circles have been the dominant cultural expression for most of human history.[9]

Only in recent centuries has humanity become obsessed with secondary social circles. The Industrial Age and its need for large work groups have contributed to this culture shift. Modernity in general has created the large metanarratives of reason, Hegelian dialectic, Marxism, communism, and the consumer culture. However, the demise of cultural metanarratives is upon us, and with it a hunger for community on a local level is emerging.[10] Simply stated, the world is tired of being served by systems; people want to go back to social circles where their needs are met in a familial way. Systems may have governed modernity, but community governs postmodern values.[11] Our younger church leaders are hearing this yearning for community.

Present churches find themselves very confused when attempting to define what kind of social structure they are. The church-growth theory, with its secondary sociological measurements, such as numerical growth, age-group programs, and people maintenance systems, has blurred the lines. Small churches function as a family, with the pastor and spouse at the familial center, meeting the needs of the group; large churches function as a city with a staff and set of systems managing the needs of the people. However, most churches are somewhere in the middle, feeling an inner impulse to be familial but also feeling guilty if they do not bring best practice systems to their church. "Creating improper intersections between primary and secondary culture generates unintended consequences of dysfunction like mafia, gangs, and local political machines," said Rah. "Each of these are family connections used to advance secondary systems."[12] Many churches are feeling the frustration of this intersection.

Deciding which social structure to align with is based on several factors, but the greatest factor is the size of the group. Historically, people have gathered in groups of 150 at a time. Author and speaker Malcolm Gladwell referred to this as the "rule of 150."[13] For example, in twenty-one hunter-gatherer societies, the average village had 148.8 people; most military fighting units are under 200; the Hutterite communities of the sixteenth century grew no larger than 150 by design; and John Wesley collected people into communities of about 150.[14] The numerical line between organic sociologies and secondary sociologies seems to be 150 people. It is interesting that the first church-growth barrier occurs when a group approaches 200 in attendance; it is the place where the attenders must stop accepting ministry from a pastor at the familial center and start accepting ministry from a staff and the systems of the organization. I propose that not every group should feel obligated to punch through to a secondary social structure. In fact, after fifty years of church-growth theory, the vast majority of Americans are still well below 150 in attendance. Maybe it is time to stop feeling guilty about that and, instead, follow Jacob Hutter's and John Wesley's lead to continue opening up organic-sized church plants.

The apostolic era reveals a church that was an organic social structure. "How else could a thousand Christians in AD 40 number thirty-four million by AD 350? Conversions occurred along relational networks; believers' care for their urban neighbors during hard times, and the close-knit community led many to convert to Christianity."[15] News about this compassionate primary culture community spread quickly over the existing secondary structures of the Roman Empire.[16] Church leaders would be well-advised to shake off the pressure of the church-growth message and embrace the organic social construct again in the manner of our apostolic fathers. To again offer a compassionate primary culture community to our neighborhoods is a very good thing.

Doing "Small" Well

Jesus used the metaphor of salt to demonstrate how the gospel is supposed to affect everything around it. The practical use of salt in Jesus' day was to season and preserve food. Thus, the metaphorical use by Christ was to instruct his followers to season and preserve society from the decay that abounds in the world. However, not all salt is able to soak into its intended object equally. For instance, rock salt cannot immerse as easily into a steak as can liquid salt. Most Christian preaching, programs, and ecclesiology are like rock salt, and they find it difficult to soak into this post-Christian nation. Congregation-based constructs are social clusters that gather people around the homogeneous unity principle (HUP) with people who already feel a kinship with the personality of the group. Rock salt is a good image for the congregation-based construct, but our secularizing nation is not interested in congregation sociologies as much as a few decades ago. "We tend to build our building and expect the lost to come to us. Our own communities have demonstrated clearly that they will not walk into our churches."[17] However, an organic approach, where the gospel is no longer fused to an imposing social cluster, can find many opportunities. An organic church construct might look like this:

- familial rather than organizational
- team rather than hierarchal
- interactive rather than performance-based gatherings
- relational rather than programmatic
- incarnational rather than attractional

The common denominator in these continuum shifts is that they are all moving in the direction of simpler.

There is a growing trend toward doing "small" well. The Foursquare denomination is presently developing Simple Church cohorts based on Thom Rainer's book by the same name, to help their leaders learn to do small well. It is their response to the shifting times and the need to walk away from complex church systems. Yet many groups and leadership streams are still assuming mega-church structures and futures. "Barna and Rainer have predicted the demise of the megachurch and the rise of the home church."[18] This is a genuine possibility that we must face. Our world is liqui-dating many of its constructs in these decades. "The symbol of the past age was the Berlin Wall; the symbol of our age is the web."[19] The wall versus the web; these are interesting images of the times. Structures that hovered over the past are liquefying right before our eyes. The congregation-based church is also a social construct of the Enlightenment, and it is starting to liquefy too. The rock salt forms of church are declining; the liquid salt forms of church are rising as an increasing number of leaders are learning to do small well. Images of relational churches seeping into their neighborhoods are eclipsing the images of programmatic churches.

A Focused Mission

Jesus offered another important metaphor in Matthew 5:14, when he called us to be "the light of the world—like a city on a hilltop that cannot be hidden." Light is an intensive thing with a singular mission. Its only job is to dispel darkness quickly—at the speed of light. The organic church is like light; it can move quickly into human need, it holds a simple mission, and it is able to focus all of its attention and intensity on that mission. Congregation-based struc-tures are diffused by nature; they must do many things well to keep people's needs met. Similar to salt, all light is not the same. Stadium lights have the ability to radiate into a general area, whereas laser light can bring the candlepower of a thousand stadium lights down to the size of a pinpoint and surgically remove a cataract from an eyeball. There is a big difference between the two forms of light.

We have had decades of generalized Christianity where everyone in the group defines for themselves how their expression of Christ is going to be lived out each week. Some content themselves to do random acts of kindness and call it Christlikeness; others grab a church task, such as ushering; still others do nothing at all because they feel they are doing enough to just show up on Sunday mornings. These forms of church engagement are similar to stadium lights; they create a generalized warm glow of Christianity. However, the secular worldview has pressed itself into the American psyche, leaving our neighbors unappreciative of the generalized warm glow created by passive Christian expressions. What our neighbors need now are a thousand expressions of Christ flowing from a church with a well-developed mission and with laser-like intentionality. Church consultant Ron McManus said, "This is not rocket science. Stop at nothing to get your people engaged in strategic mission every week. That's the one big thing that separates stalled churches from growing ones."[20] To focus people, time, and resources in intentional mission engagements is at the heart of many denominations' turn-around efforts. "If you took time to investigate effective churches across America large or small, you would discover each has a significant well-focused mission. They know what business they are in."[21]

God has sovereignly chosen to work through strategic thinking to accomplish his divine will on earth. Only 20 percent of America's 367,000 churches actively pursue strategic planning.[22] A group that is capable of pursuing a strategic plan is also capable of focus. However, focusing on a particular mission with laser-like intentionality comes with a cost: complacent people start resisting the increased sacrifice, and long-standing church members attempt sabotage efforts. New church plants with a singular mission approach will be questioned. "Churches started from the '50s thru '70s will undoubtedly question the legitimacy of many of the churches that are planted by the year 2010 or later based on the forms they use," said Malphurs.[23] This demonstrates the distance between the cherished vision of congregation-based values and the emerging vision of mission-based values.

Focused, mission-centric redemption plans cannot be initiated by a single act, but rather, they are installed by doing many things over and over, little by little, until the supply line is functional, and a redemptive flow of people coming to Christ begins. Author and business consultant Jim Collins stated it this way: "There is no single defining action, no grand program, no killer innovation, no solitary lucky break, just a process that is relentlessly pushed, turn upon turn like a huge flywheel, building momentum until the point of breakthrough."[24] Staying focused on a single mission and the few actions that propel that mission is the discipline of the organic church. This way of thinking requires more than the generalized soft glow of popular Christian expression; it requires a laser-like focus and bold mission intentionality. The organic church has the ability to keep itself free for a singular mission. Christianity is a global rescue project, and each church has a unique role in that rescue mission, a focused role.

A Simplified Conversion

The congregation-based church offers a rather complex conversion. The church of Jesus is called to offer people a conversion from the self-directed life to the Christ-directed life. However, congregation-based constructs unintentionally add a layer into the conversion process. Congregation-based churches are an alternate society that is different from common social constructs. Accordingly, for someone to come to Christ in a congregation-based church, he or she must navigate the dual transitions of a conversion to Christ and a conversion to the alternate society of the church; he or she must transition into Christianity while at the same time transitioning into "churchianity." This is a lot of conversion to require of a person. Every church leader knows this dual transition is occurring because of the pressure he or she feels from members to make a new person not only a good Christian, but also a good church person. Most pastors probably find it tougher to help new people through the church-person conversion than the Christian conversion.

The staff at Saint Aldates Church in Oxford, United Kingdom, reported that they commonly have two hundred people attend their dinner-based Alpha course, but few if any ever transition into the main worship gatherings after the Alpha series is over; they come once but do not come again.[25] It appears that people are more comfortable navigating the Christian conversion than the church-person conversion.

Organic approaches remove most of the church-person conversion from the transformation process. The dinner church approach removes the church-person conversion altogether and sets one free to focus on the Christ-conversion alone. Everyone eats dinner and understands the dinner table sociology, so no social conversion is needed. The dinner church provides a simplified conversion path.

Ignoring Some Things

The organic church needs permission to ignore some things, beginning with lifestyle issues in people trying to make their way toward Christ. In Matthew 13, Jesus told a parable about a farmer who planted a field, only to have an enemy come and plant weeds among the good seed. When the workers saw this, they assumed it would be their task to pull the weeds. To their surprise, the farmer stopped them because he did not want them uprooting the good plants in their attempts to remove the weeds. Further, the farmer instructed them to focus on nurturing the good seed and leave the weeds for the harvesters to separate out at a later time (vv. 24–30). This story reveals a human instinct to pull weeds even if it costs the health of the good seed. The American church finds itself in need of permission to ignore the weeds in the lifestyles of lost people and, instead, focus their efforts on nurturing the gospel as it grows in their understanding. The theme of inclusion creates a challenge for those who draw a thick line between the saint and the sinner and feel a need to patrol that line as a matter of Christian duty; however, this did not seem to be a challenge for Jesus. He was a friend of sinners and was criticized for eating with them (Luke 15:2).

The Reformation era created a template in our discipleship and manners of spiritual formation that has caused us to be far too obsessed with weeds. Most Christians are more focused on a homosexual's lifestyle than on his hearing an invite toward Christ. This is true for many lifestyle choices that secular people have adopted and normalized. If the church is going to once again become effective at bringing American people to faith, they must stop obsessing over the weeds in their neighbors' lifestyles and start obsessing over the divine invite that is trying to form in their neighbors' hearts. Today's church has become obsessed with the weeds for good reason; we were taught to think that way. Five hundred years ago, when John Calvin crafted the penal-substitution metaphor of atonement, many things were set in order. After all, the penal-substitution explanation of salvation is provable in the book of Romans. However, to broad brush penal substitution across everyone at all times puts some things into disorder. While it works well to motivate the already-saved toward holiness, it does not work well in creating a tone that helps the secularized person hear the invite of Christ. We can understand why Calvin, a lawyer by training, would cast an imagery of salvation as a courtroom drama that starts by naming the charge against a person (the penal portion), and then ends with Christ taking our place and being led out of the courtroom in handcuffs (the substitution portion). However, the overtone of this metaphor focuses on a person's sin; it is punishment-centric in tone.

Contrast this to the metaphor of atonement used by the apostles: the ransom metaphor that Irenaeus penned in AD 140. This picture of salvation is also provable in the book of Romans, and yet it creates the tone of a generous Savior who is willing to pay a large sum to free a person who is being victimized and oppressed.[26] The generous Savior metaphor is very different from a punishment-centric explanation of salvation. It is interesting to note that both Jesus and Paul used both approaches with different audiences. When Jesus was speaking to the woman caught in the act of adultery, he was very protective of her in ransom-like fashion; however, when he was confronting the Pharisees for their judgmental religiosity, he was very blunt in pointing out their sin. When Paul was speaking to the Athenians, who had a very secularist mind-set, he offered a very inviting and generous God to them; yet, when he was speaking to the Corinthians, who were embarrassing the poor who had shown up for the Communion meal by eating and drinking in front of them without including them, he was punishment-centric in his address to them and told them they were doing more harm than good.

There is a time for a punishment-centric conversation and there is a time for a generous-Savior conversation, and the latter is the explanation of salvation that lost people need to hear. In recent centuries, the church has courted the notion that the penal-substitution explanation is the only true gospel. That would sure be news to the Christians of the apostolic era. Yet, today many believe that if they are not pulling the weeds of wrong behavior in others, they are not being good examples of Christ. Actually, the opposite is true. After all, it was Jesus who told us to ignore the weeds and nurture the seed.

Another result of the Reformation construct that makes it almost impossible for today's Christians to ignore weeds is apologetics, which is the debate format of systematic theology. While there is great reason to appreciate a systematic understanding of the components of theological truth, it is not best served when it creates such arrogance in a Christian that he or she cannot listen to a secularist explain what he or she believes without argumentation. Further, while apologetics serves a good purpose of strengthening one's faith, it is usually not best to use it to win debates with the unsaved. Both systematic theology and apologetics are the grand-children of the Enlightenment more than they are the servants of the historic gospel. Rationalist and evidentialist apologetics was born largely in the 1970s, but has fallen on hard times these days, says transformational architect Ron Martoia.[27] In this day, when a growing percentage of Americans are adopting a secularist worldview, winning a truth argument means losing a neighbor's attention and, subsequently, his or her desire to hear the invite of Christ. Apologetics has created an argumentative tone in American Christianity and left us with the reputation that we are judgmental, homophobic, and arrogant in our views. Pastor Dan Kimball said, "Based on outside observations of Christians, there's no way I would want to become one of them either."[28] Apologetics has caused the unintended consequence of getting contemporary Christians overly focused on the border between the saved and the unsaved. Correspondingly, the overtones of exclusion are drowning out the overtones of a generous Savior, and the weeds are distracting the body of Christ from nurturing the seeds of the divine invite in the hearts of our neighbors.

Another constraint of the congregation-based church construct that has created an undue focus on weeds is church membership. These arbitrary lines create a disruption in the flow of one's journey toward Christ and focus everyone's attention on whether or not a person has transformed in certain behavioral areas to match the rest of the group. Leith Anderson, president of the National Association of Evangelicals, challenged this model. "Church membership is not biblical terminology," he said.[29]

Christ redeems aspects of people's lives in different ways and in different times. To draw a uniform border and then declare that everyone above that border is "in," and everyone below that border is "out" was not an apostolic activity, yet it has become common-place in congregation-based churches. Their need to create a border to determine good church people has overwhelmed the singular gospel goal of protecting the seed at all costs. This practice, no matter how godly it appears, has focused the eyes of the church person on everyone else's weeds. Church membership has made it almost impossible for believers to ignore weeds and practice Jesus' parable of focusing on the fragile invite to Christ that is quietly growing in the souls of our neighbors.

Similarly, even the Sinner's Prayer empowers the arbitrary line of who is in and who is out. It is interesting that there is no record that Luther, Calvin, or Augustine ever invited anyone to pray the Sinner's Prayer.[30] For that matter, neither did Christ, or Paul, or Peter, or James, or any writer in Scripture. According to Daniel Tomberlin, the Sinner's Prayer was not developed until the Great Awakening of the eighteenth century, "when sinners were called to the 'mourner's bench' to cry out for forgiveness. Since then, the altar call has been a fixture in most Evangelical worship services."[31]

Think of it: the church of Jesus made it eighteen hundred years without the Sinner's Prayer.

Reggie McNeal believes we are coming into a day when church membership in a local congregation will no longer be a primary spiritual activity for the followers of Jesus.[32] Perhaps we are moving into a time when it will be easier for Christians to ignore the weeds while they nurture the fragile seed of the divine invite that is softly calling in the soul of every one of our neighbors.

Summation

The Toyota Camry has been one of the highest-selling cars in America since 2010. However, if you're planning a trip to the top of a snow-capped mountain, a Camry might not be the vehicle of choice; a Sno-Cat, with tracks—the type of vehicle ski resorts use—might be better. Destination, not popularity, determines the vehicle. The church ought to trade the congregation-based sociology and choose an ecclesial construct more fit for the secularized snow peaks we now need to overcome; it might be a good thing to sell the Camry.

Organic approaches are different from the congregation-based constructs that we have become accustomed to. Organic churches are familial, unpretentious, focused on a singular mission, easily absorbed into society, and—most of all—dedicated to a simple path toward Christ. Organic Christianity is serious about the rescue mission and its specific role in that mission. Organic churches are positioned for mission like no other ecclesial structure, and they will not rest until they are seeping the gospel into their neighbor-hoods, winning a victory for their neighbors.[33]

CALLING FORTH
MISSION-BASED CHRISTIANS

*Transforming Go-to-Church Christians
into Missionary Christians*

Proclamation-based constructs shape people in certain ways; some are great expressions of Christianity and some are not so great. John Dyer, director of web development for Dallas Theological Seminary, believes that there are two stories at work in society: the first is how humans shape the world using tools, and the second is how those tools, in turn, shape us.[1] The proclamation-based template was a tool that was shaped five hundred years ago by the reformers for the purpose of getting the newly available Scriptures into the lives of Christians. Further, it was developed in a time when Europe was completely Christianized.[2] Thus, it had no missiology to speak of because it did not need one. This background reveals that the proclamation-based construct was strong at helping Christians learn the Scriptures, but weak at pouring its Christians out into the redemptive mission. Presently, the proclamation-based construct is functioning according to its original design and is shaping its people in predictable ways.

According to Rev. Alton Garrison, 80 percent of church members believe that church is to "provide a place where Christians can share God's love with one another."[3] These inward attitudes are the predictable result of the proclamation-based construct. Gandhi noticed this diversion and stated, "I like your Christ, but I do not like your Christians; they are so unlike your Christ."[4] How is it that we as Christ's people have become almost unrecognizable? The proclamation-based template has assisted this dilution. Church campuses can become a buzz of activity, but often miss the right kinds of activity, the kind that Christ repeated over and over again when he was on earth. Many campus-centric churches are like what leadership guru Deborah Ancona referred to as "sizzle without the steak."[5] The American church finds itself in an odd intersection transforming "go-to-church Christians" into "missionary Christians." Alton Garrison worded it this way: "We must take consumers and make them servants."[6]

Jesus gave several compelling parables that shared a common theme of calling people into the redemptive mission of the kingdom. These age-old stories still pull at the heartstrings and prompt a mission-centric lifestyle for any serious follower. They also prompt a mission-based way of doing church that is not easily merged with the proclamation-based way of doing church. What follows is a meditation on Jesus' stories and recurring actions that were intended to shape a missionary heart in his people.

Divine Priority

In Luke 15, Jesus told a three-layer story about the lost sheep, the lost coin, and the lost son. The common strand was that something important became lost, and the people involved were willing to reorganize their schedules to engage in a serious and intentional search. The inescapable meaning for the gospel is that searching for lost people is a higher priority than everything else.

This parable also reveals that searching for the lost is an emotional event. We can feel the deep concern as the shepherd heads out into the night, the desperation of the woman feverishly sweeping her house as if her next meal depended on finding that coin, and the restless father searching the horizon in hopes of seeing his son coming over the hill. We then revel in the jubilant emotion when the shepherd scoops up the lost lamb, the woman holds her lost coin firmly in her hand, and the father embraces his son and cries into his shoulder. Searching for the lost is emotional stuff. If we ever lose our emotion of what it feels like to be lost and cease to revel when days of mourning are replaced by days of rescue, we will soon forget to make the lost our first priority.

In the seventeenth century, a contemplative church leader named Ignatius Loyola observed that Christ offers four invitations to his followers through Scripture. These have become known as the Four Calls of Christ:[7]

- the call of love
- the call to the kingdom
- the call to suffer with Christ
- the call to tie the mystical knot with Christ—the divine union

Christ is intentional about inviting his people into his redemption mission. After first experiencing Christ's love, we are then called to engage in the life and goals of the kingdom and willingly suffer with Christ in pursuing those redemption goals. Then we enter into such a union with the Savior that whatever he pursues in his Messianic role on the earth, we would be at his side. These last calls shift us from inviting Christ into our lives and, instead, he begins inviting us to live in his life. If we are living in Christ's life, we are living on the bleeding edge of redemption. These progressive calls move us more and more to the great priority—that the lost be sought above all else.

Proclamation-based churches struggle to keep their eyes on the great priority: the rescue of the lost. Though most churches begin with a focused redemption mission in mind, research on the life cycle of churches reveals that a group's original sense of mission usually starts to fade within eight years.[8] The needs of the attenders start to eclipse the needs of the lost, and the rescue project fades.

Archbishop William Temple stated that the church is to be the only society in the world that exists for the benefit of those who are not its members.[9] However, proclamation-based constructs war against that outward vision and insist on diverting resources toward the present attenders. Even though many groups try to maintain some outreaches, they become what Alan Johnson referred to as the unwanted stepchild of the church, and all too quickly only a few people actually show up for outreach events.[10] Any group that uses the majority of its financial and human resources on the insiders is in need of a transformation.

Mission-based churches, however, find it very natural to stay in rescue mode. While proclamation-based people usually select their church based on how much they like the gatherings and programs, mission-based people select their church on the basis of that group's redemption mission. Thus, the glue that forms and binds the group together is their particular mission. Their ongoing missionary identity and weekly redemption-oriented schedule continually confirm and reconfirm the mission-centric identity of that church.

Not all groups who consider themselves missional are mission-based churches. Of course, any church who gives as little as one dollar to a missionary in a year is statistically a missional church, but that does not mean that those people have adopted a missionary identity and are showing up each week to engage in a rescue mission. Any group that talks more about their gatherings than about their Great Commission efforts is not a mission-based group. And conversely, any group that is enthralled with their unique role in the global rescue mission and talks very little about their gatherings is probably a focused group of missionaries in a mission-based church.

Many churches would be taking a big step forward to admit that they are not prioritizing the lost with their time, their talk, their emotion, or their money. Such a confession could be a great day for them and lead them to a much-needed transformation to become a mission-based church with missionary Christians. We must never forget that above all else, Christianity is a rescue project.

A Theology of Church Closures

At some point, leaders must consider the theology of church closures. While this may sound foreboding, such honesty is needed to inspire the necessary soberness for a church to repent and recommit to the priority of the lost. In Jesus' parable of the barren fig tree (Luke 13:6–9), it was determined that the unfruitful tree needed a root treatment to become fruitful. While Jesus never told the end of the story, the point is plain: he expects his people and his churches to be fruitful in replication. This is a parable of divine expectation. An interesting warning is served to any church that remains fruitless: Christ himself will pluck it from the garden. While that sounds harsh, it is clear. Jesus expects effectiveness from his people in the redemption mission.

The growing multitude of churches that have closed in recent years were probably not effective at soul winning before their closure. In the Northwest Ministry Network, seventy churches have closed in the past few years. This is troubling to many people's faith. How can a church that feels the presence of the Lord every week be forced to close their doors? Darrell Guder gave a great answer when he stated that the benefits of salvation are separate from the call to become Christ's witnesses.[11] The problem of fruitlessness is not that we have lost Christ's presence; it is that we have ignored Christ's call for us to be effective witnesses among our neighbors.

This parable promises that before any church is plucked, root treatments will be given to them. But what does that mean? I believe it means that a fully formed understanding of salvation will be offered to that group. The call to salvation is twofold: the first is a call to his table of benefits, and the second is to be a soul winner and work the harvest. A church that is redemptively fruitful has a majority of their people who have answered the second call with a convincing yes. Conversely, the church that is fruitless is suffering from a majority of their group that has only answered yes to the first call into salvation and then cut Jesus off mid-sentence as he was asking them to be his soul winners.

Martin Luther claimed that we all have two conversions; the first is to come out of the world and the second is to go back into the world with the gospel.[12] Accordingly, those who only show up for Sunday mornings are following the dictates of their partial salvation; people can do this quite easily because in their minds they have never agreed to be a soul winner for Christ. To churches that are filled with this kind of believer, Christ finds ways to send evangelists and apostles to dig around their roots and call them to engage in the rescue of the lost. If after many prodding efforts a church continues to hoard the benefits of salvation among themselves and ignore the call to establish a redemption plan for their church, a day will come when they start their slide toward closure. It is a social law that is as natural as gravity; a lack of redemptive effectiveness will turn into a lack of new faces, which will then turn into attrition, which will turn into a lack of finances, and finally will turn into closure. Christ himself will allow this natural demise. An accurate theology of church closure creates a clear expectation and the necessary motivation to help any stalled group get serious about their turnaround efforts. Christ expects redemptive effectiveness from all of his churches. Church leaders may want to make a note of that.

Instructions for Empty Churches

The parable about the great banquet that Jesus told in Luke 14:16–24 offers a great insight for churches that are already stalled and declining. There is an interesting backdrop to this parable because Jesus consciously retold a story in the Palestinian Talmud of a tax collector named Bar Maayan, who gave a banquet for the city counselors; when they refused to come, he gave orders that the poor should come and eat the food.[13] This likely had interesting implications for the religious leaders who were listening to Jesus because it inferred by association that a despised tax collector understood something that they did not.

The lesson for gospel leaders in this story is incredibly simple: if our ministries are not filled to capacity, drop down to the next socioeconomic level. The leaders of Jesus' day were making the same mistakes as many leaders today; they were focusing on the upper class. The American church, especially Pentecostalism, was born among the poor, but for some reason we took "the Good News [for] the poor" that Jesus spoke of in Matthew 11:5, and crossed the tracks to pursue the skinny and beautiful people of middle- and upper-class America. Many churches now boast some of the most beautiful and desired crowds of any denomination. While it is a significant achievement to reach any people for the gospel, it is not the same achievement Jesus would have likely pursued. We have targeted a group that our Master never targeted. That should give us pause.

This parable becomes even more important in a day when 85 percent of our middle-class, family-based, congregation-centric churches are stalled and declining.[14] The common idea among church leaders is that Paul's writings are the place to find the instructions for church leadership. I suggest that Jesus would never commission his church without giving instructions of his own for their continuance, especially when they are struggling. In the Gospels, Christ gave the priority for his church: to seek the lost. He also offered the scorecard for his church: he would close them if they did not win souls. Further, he told the church what to talk about: the good news. Now, in this parable, he gives instructions to his church if they should ever find themselves in an ineffective season: they should drop down to feed the poor until their ministries are full to overflowing again.

This parable not only directs the ineffective church toward the poor, but also directs us to cook feasts for the poor. Numerous times in Scripture, Christ conjoined the dinner table, the poor, and the gospel; it was a favorite approach of his. It is little wonder why the Acts church was quick to show up as a dinnertime church. The dinner church has a very natural way of responding to the "least of these" (Matthew 25:40); it provides a way for Christians to sit down with the lost, feed the hungry, include the lonely, and tell the good news about Christ. Banquets and feasts for the poor are a great way for any stalled church to get its redemptive momentum back. L. John Bueno, executive director of Assemblies of God World Missions, said, "The kingdom of God should never settle into the relaxed and comfortable position of existing for its own purposes. Let us ask God for imaginative and creative ways of doing His work and look for the new frontiers."[15] I would propose that any stalled church take this parable at face value and consider organic approaches, like cooking feasts for the poor. It will lead to some new frontiers.

Replicating the Works of Christ

The fastest path to a missionary Christian identity is to commit to replicate the works that Jesus did when he was on earth. Doing the works of Christ is the working definition of Christlikeness, and serves as the central goal of discipleship. Most people today regard discipleship as ingesting large amounts of scriptural knowledge, discipleship classes, and discipleship materials. This knowledge-based discipleship creates people who know the creeds and can recite the verses, but lack the ability to reenact the deeds of Christ. The goal of this kind of discipleship is values-based Christlikeness. While it has certain strengths, it can leave a person unpracticed in the actual behaviors of Christ in his or her daily life.

I would propose a more pragmatic definition of discipleship: behavior-based Christlikeness. After all, the etymology of the term *Christian* means Christ's followers doing life as Christ did his life. This cannot be accomplished by memorizing scriptural information about Christ; it can only be accomplished by actually practicing the behaviors of Christ that we see Christ performing in the Gospels. This praxis approach to discipleship is the difference between the systematized discipleship of proclamation-based churches and the organic discipleship of mission-based churches. Engaging forthrightly in the good works of Christ is discipleship formation. Look at the emphasis on good deeds (printed in bold type here for emphasis) in the New Testament:

- "In the same way, let your **good deeds** shine out for all to see, so that everyone will praise your heavenly Father." (Matt. 5:16)
- "They share freely and give generously to the poor. Their **good deeds** will be remembered forever." (2 Cor. 9:9)
- "So, my dear brothers and sisters, this is the point: You died to the power of the law when you died with Christ. And now you are united with the one who was raised from the dead. As a result, we can produce a harvest of **good deeds** for God." (Rom. 7:4)
- "For we are God's masterpiece. He has created us anew in Christ Jesus, so we can **do the good things** he planned for us long ago." (Eph. 2:10)
- "He gave his life to free us from every kind of sin, to cleanse us, and to make us his very own people, totally committed to doing **good deeds**." (Titus 2:14)
- "So you see, faith by itself isn't enough. Unless it produces **good deeds**, it is dead and useless." (James 2:17)
- "Tell them to use their money to do good. They should be rich in **good works** and generous to those in need, always being ready to share with others." (1 Tim. 6:18)
- "Let us think of ways to motivate one another to acts of love and **good works**. And let us not neglect our meeting together." (Heb. 10:24–25)

This last example makes it clear that inspiring good works was the primary goal of gathering as a church. Such a goal would create significant shifts for many weekend service-planning teams.

In the Christian context, our list of good works comes not from ourselves, but from our Master. When Jesus walked on the earth, he only did a few things with his time, but he did those few things repeatedly. We can observe behavioral Christlikeness by observing Jesus' recurring behaviors in the Gospels. While there is not a direct correlation between the amount of Gospel scriptures and the actual percentage of time spent on a particular behavior, there is at the very least a casual correlation that is worthy of meditation. Below are the recurring works of Christ and the percentage of passages in the Gospels that are devoted to revealing those behaviors without counting the retelling of any of the events in the subsequent Gospels:

1. Prayer and spiritual formation: 6 percent (118 verses)
2. Healings and miracles: 8 percent (170 verses)
3. Confronting judgmental religion: 8 percent (166 verses)
4. Breathing comfort: 9 percent (181 verses)
5. Answering questions: 9 percent (182 verses)
6. Spending time with the marginalized: 11 percent (216 verses)
7. Talking about the kingdom: 20 percent (421 verses)
8. Showing others how to do his works: 29 percent (583 verses)

This overview of how Jesus spent his days reveals some interesting things. First, the amount of time Jesus spent in prayer and spiritual formation was not extreme. Many shrink away from pursuing Christlikeness because they think he prayed all the time, but they have to go to work. Actually, Christ only spent a moderate amount of his time in prayer and spiritual formation, based on verse averages. That level of spiritual development is within most people's reach.

Second, Jesus' time spent performing healings and miracles causes other people to shrink away from attempting to replicate his behaviors. While Christ-followers may not possess the ability to heal everyone like Jesus did, they can at least pray for it. David Godwin, a missionary to South America, noted that the more he prayed for healing, the more healing occurred.[16] Behavioral Christlikeness bids followers to offer the prayer of healing when the opportunity arises. In so doing, some will be healed and everyone will feel cared for.

Third, a significant amount of Jesus' time was spent with the marginalized populations. This leads to a prickly question: Can a person be a good example of Christ and not spend some of his or her routine time with the poor? If one is only pursuing values-based Christlikeness, he or she would likely answer yes. If, however, one were pursuing behavioral Christlikeness, the answer would be no. It is not possible for us to be good examples of Christ and spend our time in a manner vastly different from his. Nor can we be good examples of Christ and routinely ignore many of the things that he repeated. The same is true for the other behaviors on the works-of-Christ list, like breathing comfort and speaking out against judgmental religiosity from time to time.

It could be argued that Jesus engaged in only eight salvific behaviors, and that he performed them over and over again for our benefit—so that we would replicate them. I would propose that these repeating works of Christ comprise the actual definition of Christianity and the goal of all discipleship. Praxis discipleship, which starts by engaging in the behavior first and then affecting the heart and mind, is a very organic approach to Christlike formation.

The first church clearly picked up Christ's salvific behaviors and made them their own. Following Jesus' ascension, he sent the Paraclete to empower and enable his people to shoulder the redemption mission he left behind. Thus, Pentecost not only marks the birth of the church, but also marks the empowerment to do the works of Christ so as to build his church. In the Johannine picture, the Holy Spirit comes at baptism and then manifests himself in the community through the healing gifts.[17] While in some parts of the world, the gift-of-tongues acts are seen as the pinnacle of the Pentecostal experience, other parts of the world assume that the greatest empowerments are the ones more useful in the redemption mission (like the gift of healing). While many in this camp do not exclude tongues, they do more greatly value the gifts that readily help the evangelistic task. Paul himself, though he said he spoke in tongues more than any of the people to whom he wrote (1 Corinthians 14:18), still downplayed the use of tongues in favor of the gifts that helped sinners (see 1 Corinthians 14:5, 24–25).

David Lim, pastor of Grace Assembly of God in Singapore, noted that Americans associate Pentecostalism with tongues, whereas in his home city of Singapore and elsewhere in the East, the community associates Pentecostalism with healing. He concluded that Western Christianity emphasizes a gift that evangelism cannot use.[18] Interestingly, almost all conversions occurring around the world, especially south of the equator, occur as a direct result of a miracle or healing.[19] When Jesus walked the earth, his use of the Holy Spirit's gifts most often centered on healing as compared to other empowerments. Similarly, the spiritual activities of the Acts church reveal that they expressed the Spirit's power more often in the direction of healing than of other gifts. This church held power—healing power. A verse-by-verse overview of the book of Acts reveals that healing, signs, and wonders significantly outnumber all other Holy Spirit empowerments.[20] Just as Jesus' primary activities in the Gospels focused on eating and healing, so, too, did his first followers in the book of Acts.[21]

For the works of Christ to begin to define a disciple's life, that individual must be practiced in a Great Commission environment. Proclamation-based churches struggle to provide Great Commission environments in their weekly schedule amid their other services and Bible studies. The mission-based churches, however, live for Great Commission environments and enter them naturally and easily. Thus, practicing the works of Christ on a weekly basis is a natural result of church. Even more notable is the dinner church, where almost all of the works of Christ are exercised every week. Spending time with the marginalized, breathing comfort, praying for healing and miracles, and talking about Christ and his kingdom are all commonplace around the dinner tables.

Theologian Miroslav Volf reported that early believers used to baptize new converts by speaking a phrase over them after they came out of the water: "Another Christ, sent to the world."[22] I find that phrase to hold the deepest meaning of Christian discipleship. We are not called to know the verses about Christ brought on by the discipleship systems of our churches, but we are called to spend our time in similar ways as our Master spent his time. After all, we are each "another Christ."

Safeguarding New Vision

Transitioning from a congregant to a missionary requires embracing and pursuing a new vision. However, new visions are usually disrupting events. In Luke 5:37–39, Jesus used the metaphor of wineskins to help his church understand the dynamics of bringing change. This parable is ripe with meaning for a church that is considering a transformation. Darrell Guder contended that cultures do not stand still, but rather, they evolve and change; as Western culture moves beyond the forms of Christendom, the gospel must be translated for new cultures.[23] It is difficult for most Christian leaders to admit that America has shifted to a new culture. The Christendom and Reformation eras are fading, and the ways of doing church that were translated during those periods are fading along with them. Translation is not as much a linguistic task as a cultural alignment task.

When Jesus came, he brought a new vision of salvation, a new gospel of favor for even the poor. But his new vision evoked a negative reaction from those who were mired in the old vision of Judaism. Jesus responded with his analogy of new wine and wineskins. His new vision was the wine in his analogy, and the wineskins were his way of dispensing his wine. An early lesson from this parable is that every vision has to be housed in a human social structure just as every wine has to be housed in a wineskin.

The primary point of Jesus' story, however, was not the association between vision and the constructs that house it, but rather, the reaction new vision causes. Every new culture begs for a new gospel vision, and that, in turn, begs for a new construct to house it. Fortunately, significant culture shifts do not occur very often. Peter Drucker noted that every few hundred years throughout Western history, a sharp transformation has occurred where society altogether rearranges itself, its worldview, its social and political structures, and its key institutions; fifty years later a new world exists.[24] For church leaders who happen to be at the helm during a significant cultural shift, the work of transforming the wine and the wineskins is their leadership challenge; this happens to be one of those rare seasons.

This parable reveals the leadership challenge of bursting wineskins and vision sabotage by followers who despise a new vision because they are still longing for the old, cherished vision. However, when an old vision no longer serves the gospel to the neighbors effectively, it is dysfunctional, even if the present Christians still like it. Edgar Schein, an expert in the field of organizational development, believes that it is an ultimate act of leadership to destroy a culture when it becomes dysfunctional.[25] However difficult that may appear, it is one of the great tasks of leadership. There is always a great temptation to adopt a new mission but not change the social structure that houses it; on paper it looks possible and less painful, but Jesus' parable is clear: you do not put new wine into old wineskins.

Some interpret this passage to mean that Jesus is telling us to avoid bringing change to people so they do not burst. I suggest that the point of his analogy has little to do with preserving the wineskins and everything to do with not ruining the new wine. This is a matter of not allowing new vision to be ruined by older human structures. If a group tries to change its vision without changing its social structure, the old social structure will kill the vision, and it will be spilled onto the ground. The potential cost of trying to put new vision into old structures is the spilling of the new vision all over the ground and losing it for the kingdom of God.

I expect that most new visions in the coming years are going to be mission-based visions. Accordingly, congregation-based structures will predictably burst and spill the mission-oriented vision all over ground. Congregation-based social structures are not wineskins that can handle mission-based wine; if they are going to be useful in missionary vision, they will need to unlearn many congregation-centric values and be rebuilt as a mission-centric family of missionaries who are singularly committed to a particular redemption plan for that church.

New vision and a new church construct to house that vision is risk-oriented; however, one thing this parable does not do is instruct leaders to avoid the risk. In fact, the reason it is being told is precisely because Jesus engaged the risk for the sake of his new salvation plan. Leadership studies pioneer Warren Bennis once stated, "You must put yourself at risk regularly. If you're not scared you're not growing."[26] Transformation brings one risk after another, but do it anyway. It is the only way forward; it is the only way to new growth. Pastor Rob Ketterling tells of a time he asked God when there would be less financial risk in their church. God answered him, "Never."[27] Risk is on the horizon for every leader of every church that plans to be in business in the next fifteen years.

Creating new vision and new ecclesial constructs to house it requires dogged determination because navigating transformation is tricky. "Be dramatic," advised Aubrey Malphurs. "Take the team on a tour of the auditorium when it's empty to show them what it will look like in one or two years on Sunday morning."[28] John Kotter, an authority on leadership and change, said we need to create a strong sense of urgency, and to do so, we must take bold actions that we normally do not associate with good leadership.[29] Transformational leadership is exactly the opposite of keeping the troops calm; it is a time of motivating the group to change their wine and change the wineskins they have learned to like. Transformational leadership that outlasts bursting wineskins and vision sabotage by people longing for the old wine will require sustained determination by a few leaders at the core.

The proclamation-based construct holds a cherished vision about the Sunday morning service that binds people to the church. To replace that cherished vision with a mission-based purpose will be costly. Never mind that it is altogether scriptural and needed for the church's survival, it will still cause wineskins to burst and sabotage efforts to soar. It will take time to outlast these reactions. Jim Collins observed that it takes most businesses about four years to find a new vision that is right for them and transition the company to the point that they appreciate the change.[30] And these are people who are getting paid to be there. How much tougher is it for church people who are not paid to be there?

Collins further stated that every company that transformed effectively embraced the Stockdale Paradox and maintained unwavering faith that they could and would prevail in the end, while at the same time confronting the brutal setbacks.[31] Jim Stockdale was a US pilot who was shot down and held in a concentration camp for many years. He maintained his sanity while many of his cell mates did not because he held on to the belief that he would someday get out, though he did not know when. Dogged determination of a Stockdale nature is needed in the leadership soul of the transforming church. One day, new visions with a new church construct will be at the service of the Master again—if we faint not.

Summation

The proclamation-based construct of the reformers has served many people well in their journey of faith; however, the Reformation era is waning while a mission era is coming. The church template that formed Christ's people for the last five hundred years is being retooled before our very eyes. What this means in human terms is a transformation from proclamation-based Christianity to mission-based Christianity, and from go-to-church Christians to missionary Christians. Christ is forever inspiring mission imagery in his people and calling them to lose themselves in the divine priority of rescuing the lost. We must never forget that above all else Christianity is a rescue project.

5

PREFERRING THE POOR

A Theology of Poverty:
A Christ-Centric Approach to Society

You will always have the poor among you." Jesus uttered those words in three of the four Gospels in defense of a woman's expensive worship (see Matthew 26:11; Mark 14:7; John 12:8). However, there is a deeper assumption in these words. Most Christians read these verses as a prediction, when they are actually stating a necessity. The church needs the poor as much as the poor needs the church. The poor provide for our greatest worship; when we are adoring the poor, we are actually adoring Christ. The poor also provide for our greatest discipleship; when we respond to the poor, we are practicing the greatest expressions of Christlikeness. The poor also provide for our greatest mission; when we are lifting the poor, we are entering society through a door where we will be welcomed. The poor are not just a fact of life; they are the intended intersection for the Savior to enter the affairs of this world. That is why Jesus often repeated the refrain, "I am preaching the gospel to the poor" (Matt. 11:5, paraphrased). That was both the identifier and the method of his new redemption plan on the earth.

In wealthy America we have overlooked this foundational theology of poverty, assuming that everyone here is middle-class and well-fed. That assumption has never been true. In 2013, two out of five American families visited a food bank.[1] American cities are now reporting that 30 percent of their populations live beneath the poverty line.[2] Best-selling author Philip Yancey reported that one-third of all dog and cat food was purchased by senior citizens too poor to afford human food.[3] It is no longer valid to assume this is middle-class America; things are changing. There is a silver lining in this challenge, however. The church is getting another chance to walk through Christ's favorite societal door if we can learn to adore the poor as the most honored people in our neighborhoods. The unexpected blessing that flows from preferring the poor will be a great surprise to a great company of Christian leaders.

The Poor in Christ's Kingdom

The day Jesus went to the synagogue and read from the scroll of Isaiah 61:1–2 was his version of publishing a mission statement. He read: "The Spirit of the LORD is upon me, for he has anointed me to bring Good News to the poor. He has sent me to proclaim that captives will be released, that the blind will see, that the oppressed will be set free, and that the time of the LORD's favor has come" (see Luke 4:16–21). The line that was obviously arresting to him, because he repeated over and over again was, "preach the gospel to the poor" (Luke 4:18 KJV). The gospel and the poor are forever fused together. Christ's redemption plan is indelibly welded to the poor. In Luke 7:19–22, John the Baptist sent his disciples to ask Jesus if he was really the Messiah. Jesus told them to go back and tell John that the gospel was being preached to the poor. That was the proof Jesus offered for his Messianic identity.

Christ proved his mission statement by the way he spent his time. Eleven percent of the Gospel verses capture Jesus being with the marginalized. That should speak something very loud to the church. Further, Jesus' use of dinnertimes to embrace slaves, sinners, tax collectors, and disreputable women became a contro-versial feature of his ministry. "Many do not realize that Jesus created the parables in Luke 15 to defend his practice of welcoming sinners to his joyful eschatological supper," wrote Asbury professor

Christine Pohl. "We may reasonably assume that the context in which Jesus usually recited these parables was his controversial supper."[4] Pohl noted that it should be apparent from Scripture that Jesus' controversial suppers were a prominent and regular feature of his ministry.[5] Preferring the poor around dinner tables was one of Christ's recurring habits.

During the Last Supper, Jesus cast a vision to his disciples to make the annual Passover meal a common occurrence and, similar to the Passover tradition, to eat together around tables with brothers and strangers, remembering the Lamb, Jesus. That vision of the Passover table became the vision for the book of Acts church, whose members hosted so many dinners and talked about Christ with such continuance that it was said of them, "you have filled all Jerusalem with your teaching about him" (Acts 5:28). This Communion meal soon took on larger forms called love feasts that we read about in 1 Corinthians 11 and Jude 12: notice that the poor were present. The makeup of the Corinthian church consisted of Jewish merchants, Gypsies, Greeks, prostitutes, pagan idolaters, and the poor.[6] Christ must have been proud of his followers; his beloved poor were sitting around tables with his beloved church.

There are twenty-three hundred verses in the Bible about the poor; it is the central message of Scripture that is surpassed only by the theme of redemption.[7] Given this volume of scriptural content focused on the poor, it is interesting how the American church has held it as a minor theology. Giving preferential place to the poor is anything but a minor theology. In fact, Jesus' parable about the sheep and the goats in Matthew 25:31–46 speaks of a day when a serious separation between people will occur on the basis of one thing: how they responded to the poor. In Jesus' story those who took care of the poor, the hungry, the widow, and the prisoner were likened to sheep and given favorable standing. However, those who overlooked the poor, the hungry, the widow, and the prisoner were likened to stubborn goats and given an unfavorable status. This should be a sobering story for the American church because we have overlooked a lot of poor people in our efforts to fill our

Sunday-morning services with upper-class people. In this way, the church has jumped the tracks that Christ laid down for us.

Alan Johnson noted that statistically the church is following a missiology that places us in circumstances not of poverty but of wealth, and not of oppression but of freedom.[8] If this is true of our mission fields, it is doubly true in our own large cities; we are consistently planting churches in suburban areas while ignoring the neighborhoods where poverty abounds. This sounds scarily close to the goats in Christ's story; it would not be a foolish thing for us to be shaped by this parable and reconsider our theology of poverty. "Those who abandon everything in order to seek God know well that he is the God of the poor."[9]

The Historic Door for the Gospel

After the ascension of Christ, the church was officially in the apostles' hands. True to the example of Christ, the apostles gave the poor a preferential place in the newly forming church. In fact, the first internal conflict was over better care for the poor widows (see Acts 6). Think of it: a church fight over better care for the poor. In fact, the role of the deacon would not have emerged if the young church had not desired to provide better care for the poor. Perhaps there will come a day when the role of deacon will be won back from the boardroom and be restored to the all-important role of lifting the poor.

From that day forward, the apostolic era revealed one chapter after another where the fusion between the church and the poor became cemented. The agape feasts and the poor laundry workers were gossiping the gospel through the large cities of the Pax Romana with such fervor that the term *pagan*, which originally meant country-dweller, as noted earlier, came to refer to those who lived outside the major cities as the last ones exposed to the Christian faith.[10] When the plagues decimated many Roman cities and killed 30 to 40 percent of their inhabitants,[11] though all the doctors fled, the Christians, without regard to their own welfare, stayed behind, tending to the sick and nursing as many as two-thirds of them back to health.[12] The church made a great mark on the Roman world because of their willingness to prefer the poor and the sick. David Kinnaman of the Barna Group reported that "pagans were drawn to Christ when they saw the love of Christians. When Constantine declared Rome the Holy Roman Empire, it wasn't for political reasons as it was already Christianized; he just recognized the realities."[13] Preference of the poor led to preference of the church; that is no small consideration.

Further demonstrations of the fusion of the church and the poor have been revealed through the centuries. The Franciscans, a monastic order, and the Poor Clares, a female monastic order, took vows of poverty so they would never find themselves uncomfortable with the poor, and they developed numerous ways to support the impoverished populations. In sixteenth-century England, as much as 50 percent of the population faced grinding poverty and vagrancy.[14] This poverty set the stage for the Stranger's Friend Society, developed by John Wesley in the late 1700s, who dedicated themselves to ministry among London's urban poor.[15] Then, in the 1800s, William Booth's Salvation Army responded to London at a time when it had eighty thousand prostitutes, with a vision that everyone have at least the life of a cab horse, with shelter at night, food to eat, and work to do.[16] These are just a few of the many examples of the church exercising its theology of poverty.

Another more recent chapter in the theology of poverty is associated with the Great Awakening and the subsequent Pentecost revivals. These events all share a common thread: the church was engaged in a collective response to poverty when "the Spirit fell." To disconnect those empowering events from the preference of the poor being offered in urban settings would do injustice to the story. I suggest that the timing of the outpouring is an important factor; God sent the Spirit at those moments to both confirm the church's activities among the poor and to give greater empowerment so they could be more effective in the areas where the need was so great. It is a little disturbing that some church leaders have let the backdrop of poverty fade away from their retellings of the outpouring events. Nonetheless, the fusion between the theology of the church and the theology of poverty found a new partner—the theology of Pentecost.

Given the deep history between the church and the poor, present-day leaders would do well to interchange "mission" with "poverty alleviation" because they might be more closely linked than most think. The historic front door for the church has been the poor; the poor have enabled the rich history of the church more than any other social factor.

Primary Relevance

Lifting the poor is on a far higher plane than whether or not the guitars are perfectly tuned. Talk about being relevant in today's church world usually translates to untucked shirts, spiked hair, cool worship music, and a worship leader with a tattoo peeking out of his sleeve. The problem with the American church is that we have signed up for too small of a game; we are concerning ourselves with stylistic issues in a day when society needs big answers from big people. We might want to consider leaving behind some surface goals and, instead, engage in some primary relevance issues that are deeply concerning our neighbors. Things such as poverty, crime, and children being sucked into pornography might be more important to our neighborhoods than another Easter egg hunt.

One church in the United Kingdom studied their crime-ridden city and noted that in every neighborhood where there was a church, crime occurrences were less frequent. Then they planted a church in a high-crime area to see if the crime occurrences would decrease. To their delight, over the next year, the crime rate reduced to match the other neighborhoods with churches. They presented their research to the city, which was so impressed that they voted to include church plants into their city-expansion maps as a part of their crime-abatement plan.[17] A Harvard study credited Twelfth Street Baptist Church in Detroit, Michigan, with reducing crime in their neighborhood by more than 37 percent over three years.[18] Here in the United States, studies have revealed that church attendance is a substantial predictor of inner-city black males escaping poverty, drugs, and crime.[19] Churches can take on large issues that are on our neighbors' minds. We would do well to remember that crime-ridden and poverty-ridden neighborhoods are native territory for the church of Jesus.

In 1943, the famed psychiatrist Abraham Maslow drafted the Hierarchy of Human Needs.[20] Maslow's theory is that the first need a person must address is survival; then he or she must address a second need of security; then comes the need for validation; followed by the need to love and be loved; the final level of human need is fulfillment. In recent decades, the church has spent most, if not all, of its time meeting people on the upper tiers of human need. We have crafted lessons, sermons, and programs that speak to people's needs for validation, love, and fulfillment. However, to embrace the theology of poverty and give preference to the poor is to serve the primal levels of human need: survival and security. The Western church has been trying to enter the upper-tier doors of society when our gospel has historically entered the lower-tier doors: food for the hungry, shelter for the exposed, and protection for the vulnerable. What if churches again started pursuing the lower hierarchy of needs? Maybe the better question is this: What has been the effect on the churches that have ignored the primal needs of humanity?

There is a lesson from the church in Russia that warrants consideration. Pastor Rick Rusaw noted that when the Bolshevik Revolution occurred in 1917, the Communists did not make it illegal for the church to exist, but they did make it illegal for the church to do any good works. No longer could the church fulfill its historic role of feeding the hungry, housing the orphans, or caring for the sick. The state would handle those duties. The result? After seventy years, the church in Russia was largely irrelevant. In America we have done by default what Lenin did by diabolic design.[21] Leith Anderson offered further insight. While the Bolshevik Revolution was occurring, the leaders of the Russian Orthodox Church gathered for a conference to debate the colors for their clergy vestments.[22] I propose that the American church is at a similar intersection as the Russian church was one hundred years ago; we are spending our time on stylistic issues while ignoring our primary reason for societal relevance: lifting the poor. This has serious implications for our future. Lewis Shelton, former president of Bethany College, warned:

> I predict that in my lifetime American churches will lose their tax-exempt status. The reason tax-exempt status was granted had to do with churches caring for the marginalized. Churches were the only social safety net for the poor. In recent decades, however, churches have become teaching centers and ceased the function of responding to the poor; the government has taken over the role of lifting the poor. In the future, churches will have to prove that they are primarily engaged in poverty alleviation to maintain their tax-status.[23]

Trust me when I say, true relevance has nothing to do with cool shirts, cool hair, and cool worship music on Sunday morning. True relevance is informed by the theology of poverty.

The Invisible Poor

Most people equate poverty with homelessness, but there is another face of poverty that encompasses a large percentage of Americans and is far less visible. The church needs to spend some time considering the technical definitions of poverty. Poverty has been measured by the federal government according to poverty thresholds established in 1963 by Molly Orshansky of the Social Security Administration. Orshansky calculated the threshold of poverty by tripling the cost of a "thrifty" sack of food, then multiplying it by the number of people in a family. Those whose income falls below this threshold, known more commonly as the federal poverty line (FPL), are considered to be in poverty; the formula remains the same forty-seven years later.[24] Today, however, the average family spends far more on housing, transportation, and utilities than a family in the 1960s did.[25] Thus, the federal poverty line has gone through a necessary adjustment. Polls indicate that most American families need twice the FPL to survive in today's economy.[26] The current FPL for an individual is an annual income of $10,830, but most social organizations will give assistance for rent, utilities, child care, and health care based on the adjusted FPL or an annual income of $21,660. Thus, the technical definition of poverty is any person earning $21,660 per year or less.

It is a surprise to most church leaders to find out how many people in their neighborhoods are living below the poverty line. Using Seattle as an example, the census report reveals that in 2006, 29 percent lived below the poverty line.[27] That is almost one out of every three Seattleites who do not know where they are going to live next month or what they are going to eat tonight. That equates to 166,000 people in my city that are struggling. That number is huge. It is far larger than the homeless rate from that same period, of 8,937.[28] This is where most church leaders misread the issue. They look at Seattle and assume that poverty is the 8,937 homeless people that are visible, when it is actually 166,000 people, most of whom are invisible. Seattle's percentages are not abnormal. Even smaller cities are finding surprising percentages of their neighbors living beneath the poverty level. The church must learn to recognize poverty as something different from the homeless guy on the park bench. Even homeless populations are different than most people think; 55 percent of the homeless in our city are families with children.[29]

The faces of poverty in our country are the seniors who are eating dog food, the underemployed man who cannot get enough hours in to pay rent, and the child whose parents are homeless. Surprisingly, the largest group of people living below the poverty line is those eighteen to twenty-four years of age, single, Anglo, and female. Seattle's version of poverty is young, white, female, and educated.[30] A primary question for every church should be this: What is the face of poverty in our city?

A Deep Societal Challenge

Poverty is a chronic condition, and society struggles to find lasting solutions. Even when the federal government throws its weight into the challenge, it falters. "In 1964 President Lyndon Johnson declared unconditional war on poverty. Persons in the United States living below the poverty line dropped by one-third, but in 1970 it jumped back up to where it was before."[31] Chronic poverty is a deep challenge in our day as well. Futurologist Tom Sine reported in 2008, just before the Great Recession, that US poverty had risen for the fourth consecutive year to 12.7 percent, meaning the average impoverished family of four was trying to get by on $19,000 per year.[32] By 2016 the poverty rate had risen for the eighth consecutive year. Poverty is a chronic social ill that is not going away anytime soon.

Poverty has been a cover-up story of Western civilization and the free-enterprise system since its beginnings. We are now watching similar cover-ups playing out in the developing countries that are trying to follow our lead. "Bangladesh has erected an enormous $80 million, 8-story super mall with 2000 stores at a time when over half of people live in abject poverty with only 20 percent having electricity. Their reason is that the whole world is getting westernized; why should they be left behind?"[33]

The lesson here is that capitalism will overlook great need in its pursuit of great things. The late Nelson Mandela once warned, "We have reached a turning point in history where massive poverty and obscene inequality are terrible scourges, while the world boasts breath-taking advances in science, technology, industry, and wealth accumulation."[34] Capitalism is not capable of focusing on profits while at the same time creating opportunities for the poor. English poet and novelist John Berger argued that "the poverty of our century is unlike that of any other. This time it is not the result of natural scarcity, but of a set of priorities imposed upon the rest of the world by the rich."[35] Business leaders are not mean-spirited people; they are just keeping their companies focused on the American dream and making money. But someone needs to rise in defense of the powerless.

The church has been dulled by the values of the American dream too. Soong-Chan Rah asked a provoking question, "Why are American evangelicals so willing to overlook corporate sin like unjust economic systems that lead to poverty?"[36] The church has blended compassion and social justice into one concept when, actually, they are very different; one is about kindness and the other is about righteousness. The latter deserves a more spiritual response from spiritual people. Further dulling is evident as American churches lust for bigger and better buildings. These brick-and-mortar pursuits come with large monthly mortgages that are disabling many groups from preferring the poor who live on their blocks. As the American dream continues to rule our cities and influence our churches, it is the poor who pay the deepest price. However, a new way of thinking might be forming. Many church leaders are starting to question and grapple with the obscene amounts of money used for church aesthetics in contrast to how they deal with poverty.[37]

We live in a day when the church of Jesus could be having a profound impact on the world stage. The programs, tools, and technologies to eliminate poverty are now available to humankind.[38] World Vision president Richard Stearns wrote, "An additional 65 billion per year would be enough to lift the one billion people who live on less than a dollar a day out of their extreme poverty."[39] That means that if every American churchgoer tithed a full 10 percent rather than the average 2 percent, we would be able to solve the worst of the world's poverty three times over.[40] Imagine how stunning it would be for the world to watch the American Christians bring an end to world hunger.[41] The American churches' global opportunities are unfathomable—and all for the price of a tithe.

Extraordinary Opportunity

There is a throbbing opportunity and a compelling vision before us that wins back the idea of preferring the poor. The theology of poverty got a serious theological boost in 1974 in Lausanne, Switzerland. A convention of the world's Christian leaders assembled to consider how to correct some things that seemed to have gone awry in world Christianity. Looking at the shelf life of Christianity was revealing some disturbing trends. What began in Palestine, then jumped to the Greco-Roman world, and then jumped to the Franco-German world, and then jumped to the Scottish-British world, and then jumped to the Americas, was now jumping to the regions south of the equator, namely, South America and Africa. The disturbing part for the Lausanne organizers was the steep decline of Christianity in regions that once had been the sending centers of the gospel. After a week of prayer and dialogue, the Lausanne Congress forged a trans-formational statement: "The gospel shall never again be conceived as proclamation unwelded from social engagement."[42] This was a signif-icant shift from the proclamation-only definition of the gospel that had informed the church from the beginning of the Reformation era.

A follow-up Lausanne Congress convened fifteen years later in Manila, and it was there that the statement was captured in the phrase "the whole gospel." This phrase inferred that to only proclaim the gospel without finding a social need to serve would no longer be considered a whole expression of the gospel, but rather, only a part. The 1974 Congress opened new eyes for the church and cast a vision of both serving the gospel and proclaiming the gospel in equal measure. Thus, theological space was made for preferring the poor as a natural part of a church's weekly function. Preferring the poor was now lifted to the level of proclamation, no longer to be considered as the unwanted stepchild of a church's outreach program. It is true that most nations of the world embraced the whole gospel better than American leaders did, but perhaps our time to embrace the vision is now.

With preferring the poor back in theological style, it is a new day for church planting. Nothing will give new church plants rele-vance among urban villagers any faster than lifting "the least of these" that live in the neighborhood (Matthew 25:40). It is also a new day for discipleship. When we reach out to lift the poor, we are actually practicing the behaviors of Christ. Such praxis forms of discipleship are similar to on-the-job training that quickly forms a person's Christlikeness through practice, and is arguably a better discipleship approach. This is especially true among the "compassion generation" that makes up the twenty- and thirty-year-olds in our ministry circles.

And finally, preferring the poor also creates a new day of unexpected blessings. Proclamation-centric approaches have created some expectations in us about how people and money flow. To change our priorities to include preferring the poor is to change many other outcomes as well. I overheard a pastor and a church planter talking at a restaurant. The church planter was excited about going after the poor in his community, to which the seasoned pastor said, "Oh man, you can't build a church on people like that." I wanted to stand up and yell at the guy for his shortsighted attitude. His conclusions were based on congregation-centric results that he had observed for years. It just happens to be exactly wrong.

There are some unusual and unexpected blessings built into the spiritual path of preferring the poor. Retired Assemblies of God pastor Geoff Pickup said, "If you reach for the ones nobody wants, you will end up with the ones everybody wants."[43] To any church that determines to lift the poor in a preferential way, Jesus will give them influential people coming from unexpected places. This idea is actually built into the theories of social balancing; healthy people are drawn to care for broken people and bold leaders are drawn to vulnerable populations.[44] Not only is Jesus going to give influential people to a group with a mission to prefer the poor, but he is going to give them money and resources. This is a promise of Scripture: "If you help the poor, you are lending to the LORD—and he will repay you!" (Prov. 19:17). Calvary Church Pastor Don George said, "The law of return is infallible when a church gives to the needy."[45] The unexpected and unexplainable blessings of influential people and financial flow are coming to any church that is willing to embrace the theology of poverty.

Summation

There is a very different way of doing church, and it begins at the exact spot where Jesus began—preaching the gospel to the poor. Just as the Christiandom era followed the apostolic era, and just as the Reformation era followed the Christiandom era, the mission era is readying itself to take the helm. "A renaissance is coming," predicted humanitarian-theologian Jean Vanier. "Soon there will be a multitude of communities founded on adoration and presence to the poor, linked to the great communities of the church."[46] The mission era will be profoundly similar to the apostolic era in many ways, but none more so than the preferential treatment of the poor. "Poverty is a gift that few religious people really relish."[47] I propose that it will again be relished in the coming day of mission. In that day many will say, "We have learned the secret: that in adoring the poor, we are beholding Christ."

6

A NEIGHBORHOOD VISION

Reengaging the Six-Block Social Circle

Visions are inspired by locations far more than most leaders realize. In fact, the theology of place, which is all but lost in most leadership conversations, connects the dots between God's visions and God's calls to certain locations. Today, however, most leaders instinctively imagine the suburban world of drivers when they craft vision for their churches. This is not one of those visions; this is a neighborhood-centric vision with a theology of place foundation.

Churches were historically skilled at neighborhood thinking a hundred years ago, but by the 1940s, when automobiles were suddenly everywhere, churches changed.[1] According to historian George Kennan, the automobile became a major addiction in our culture, and wherever it advanced, neighborliness and a sense of community became impaired.[2] Along with the rest of society, the church lost its neighbor-centric perspective; leaders stopped thinking about reaching their neighborhoods and started thinking about regions and the potential attenders who live within a fifteen-minute drive of their facility. Focusing on a region creates a very different vision than focusing on a neighborhood. Neighborhoods have a particular personality; regions, on the other hand, are diffused places where multiple social circles live but seldom meet.

To understand the dinner church vision, one will have to set aside the assumptions that have been pressed into the American psyche by the automobile and, instead, recommit to a neighborhood. Pure neighborhood formation is determined by how far the people who live there are willing to walk for their services. City planners understand that neighborhoods commonly form around the sociology of the five-minute walk, which usually translates into a six-block walking circle.[3] The dinner church is all about the neighbors in the neighborhood, and spreading from neighborhood to neighborhood throughout the city. Some business plans, though they are few and far between, are neighborhood plans. For instance, Starbucks is a franchise model with a neighborhood plan that works hard to fit into the values of each location.[4] Immediate influence is given to any group that adopts the personality traits of a neighborhood. It is a missiological thing for a church in the city to be neighborhood-centric and be located in the center of the neighborhood. This is what a theology of place wins for a group. To underestimate the collective identity of the neighborhood is to underestimate the power of the dinner church vision.

Dinner Church: A Big, Neighborhood Family Table

A dinner church can enter the life of a neighborhood very quickly. The absence of familial support is very obvious in many cities, and dinner churches are welcomed because they meet that need. George Barna believes that during times of uncertainty society has survived because of our ability to cling to the relationships at home that brought us a semblance of peace and assurance; yet in this coming century the traditional comfort zone provided by the family will no longer be present.[5] Urban settings are places of raw loneliness; cities are composed of predominantly single adults, many of whom live alone and suffer from the condition known as *urban isolation*. Dinner churches restore this important social construct by creating a big, family-like table for the neighborhood. Such a church is not a Sunday event that centers on a teaching; rather, it is a dinnertime feast that centers on tables filled with food, laughter, friendship, and Christ.

When someone walks into a dinner church, hosts and hostesses greet them and direct them toward a buffet table loaded with an abundance of food that is colorfully displayed. These feasts are a full-course meal that is hand served from hot chafing dishes and carved-meat stations. The servers are Christians who feel called to be there and people from the community who have come to give back. Often, entire families are serving, with children of all ages lined up helping their parents ladle food onto plates. Guests then sit with other neighbors around tables decorated with linen clothes and enjoy the food and friendship. An acoustic guitarist fills the room with worship music, while artists paint Scripture-inspired pictures on canvas in the front of the room.

In that artistic-rich environment a hundred or more neighbors from that community sit, eat, talk, and become friends. The conversation is interspersed with laughter, and an inescapable sense of family fills the room. Toward the end of the dinner, a musician sings a worship song and one of the church planters tells an inspirational story from the life of Christ. A prayer for divine favor always follows the speaking portion. A table card instructs the guests that there will be a story about Christ and a prayer at the end for those who want to stay. Interestingly, almost everyone stays. The Christ-followers who are dispersed throughout the room, eating with the guests, often find themselves engaged in spiritual conversations and prayer for people who are at the tables. It is moving to watch. The food, the music, the artistry, the Christ story, the prayer, and the follow-up conversations all culminate into a warm and supportive experience. The most repeated comment we receive from visiting church leaders is, "This feels exactly like something Jesus would be doing." That is our highest affirmation.

For the first few months, a dinner gathering resembles a homeless meal because that is the only social construct communities have for free dinners, but then it transitions into a community meal in which the makeup of the crowd starts to resemble the makeup of the neighborhood. A final transition occurs within the year, when it moves from a community feast into a church. That final transition becomes obvious once people start referring to it as "church," calling the leaders "pastor," inquiring about what the "sermon" is going to be, demonstrating intentionality during prayer, and engaging in spiritual conversations. Based on observing these phases in six neighborhoods, the sociographic mix of the group at the one-year point is this: one-third of the group is financially challenged, one-third are alone and affected by urban isolation, and one-third are Christians and good neighbors who have shown up to lift those whose lives are not going so well. Dinner churches might be taking as many people to heaven that showed up to serve as those who showed up to be served.

After the church phase comes into maturity, many other aspects of a Christian church start to develop. People start asking to be baptized, as Jesus instructed. So, after a dinner, we take them out to one of the nearby lakes that are nestled in the city and baptize them; the other guests clap and cheer and shoot pictures on their phones. Also, those who are teachers start gathering people who want to learn more; those who are mercy-oriented start bringing hats and socks; those who are comfort-givers find more opportunities than they can count to speak encouragement into the downcast. The evangelists are drawn to those who need help getting over hurdles to faith. Another sign of maturity is that the church planters' messages start to deepen as people's spiritual hunger deepens. The room becomes filled with many expressions of Christ that are being offered in many beautiful ways. The gospel is served, cooked, played, painted, spoken, and prayed. The neighbors leave a bit more encouraged than when they came in, and the neighborhood is a little richer that night.

A Neighborhood Pastor

A further consideration about the dinner church vision is presence. Having staff parachute in and leave as soon as the tables are broken down would turn a dinner church into an event rather than Christ's people living life together with a neighborhood. A dinner church is incarnational in nature; it is a form of church that shows up in the streets, in the marketplaces, and in the neighborhood where people live their lives.[6] Thus, dinner church planters and staff actually move into the neighborhoods they are serving; this is a nonnegotiable value. Strategic-planning expert Geoff Surratt, speaking of Southside Community Church, a multi-site church that was initially planted to be a church planter, said, "One of the key ingredients in Southside's launch was the fact that the members of the core group moved into the neighborhood . . . this made all the difference."[7] Moving church planters right into the neighborhoods they are serving, having them work from coffee shops, and being available to pastor the neighborhood is no small thing.

The dinner church vision has spiritual goals for the people God gives them, but it also has social goals. One of these social goals is to help restore marginalized people to a sustainable life. A sustainable life in social terms is when a person is earning sufficient income to pay for his or her monthly expenses. For people who have lost their financial rhythm, recovering a sustainable life is very tough to do alone. For church planters living in a neighborhood, pastoring means helping people find jobs, working with business owners to create opportunities, and perhaps even helping people find housing that they can afford.

A neighborhood pastor can help people connect the dots between jobs and housing in ways many of them cannot do for themselves. Ray Bakke, a leader in the field of urban ministry, said, "We must flesh out the gospel by having Christians deliberately and strategically move into the run-down neighborhoods, living as the incarnate body of Christ."[8] While restoring some neighborhoods may appear like an impossible task, it is actually the simple things that matter.

Criminologists James Wilson and George Kelling founded the Broken Window Theory, which argued that if a window remains broken, people will conclude that no one cares and no one is in charge. Soon anarchy will spread; the idea of crime is contagious. When cities fixed up troubled neighborhoods, murders declined by two-thirds and felonies were cut in half. Wilson and Kelling's conclusion was that the key to making a difference isn't massive programs but humble, deliberate acts of cultural preservation.[9]

Church planters engage in the deliberate acts of befriending business owners and restoring people's housing and jobs. The presence of a church planter in coffee shops, talking with neighbors; on the benches, laughing with street musicians; and on the sidewalks, lifting the poor, breathes life into a neighborhood. It is divine presence at work.

If a dinner church does not have people who stay behind to live life together with the neighbors who live there, then its effect on the neighborhood is limited to a couple of hours a week. But a pastor who is seen in the shops each day helping people with real-life issues reminds every watching eye that the dinner church is there to lift the entire neighborhood. Soong-Chan Rah said he likes to just walk through his neighborhood, because the slow pace of walking allows him to observe those in pain.[10] What is missing from most neighborhoods is someone to observe the pain and try to bring "lift." Demographic profiles are no substitute for a listening presence.[11] A dinner church is encouraging to a neighborhood, but for the neighborhood to watch pastors move their families into their buildings to live among them, live with them, and lift them during their struggles—that is an encouragement of a higher order.

Neighborhood-by-Neighborhood Expansion

Most cities are built on the grid system and have quadrants. A city-wide expansion plan might include the selection of a quadrant in which to start planting the high-density neighborhoods first. This can be valuable in the sharing of resources such as cargo vans, sound equipment, food-service equipment, and personnel, such as cooks, artists, musicians, and volunteers. Another reason for quadrant thinking is that the reputation of a dinner church spreads from one nearby walking village to another. Thus, when a group goes to plant its next site, it has a ready crowd of neighbors who have been waiting for them to arrive. In Seattle, we have actually had neighbors from a nearby village send a request for us to come to their neighborhood next. How often does that happen in church planting? This is a pretty exciting way to expand church sites!

Another consideration is to choose plant locations at the beginning of an expansion plan that would serve as a learning-church site. The medical community has grasped the value of providing learning hospitals, and dinner church expansion plans would be well served to provide the same. Not all locations are good learning sites. Neighborhoods with large homeless or gang populations have different challenges than a neighborhood with a balanced mix of gender, ethnic, age, and income levels. Also, newly gentrified neighborhoods can be too tilted toward middle-class people with consumer mind-sets to serve as effective teaching locations. Neighborhoods that still have some old buildings, but with a good walking village at its center, often provide the kind of people mixes that are easy for new planters and volunteers to learn. Ask for the Holy Spirit's leading to circle some first locations that could become a good learning-church site.

Another consideration for a citywide expansion plan is to plant dinner churches in groups of four. A four-plant strategy, in which each dinner church occurs on a different night of the week, allows four church planters to work together to produce the level of leadership that is needed to stay ahead of the volunteers coming from area churches and the helpful neighbors that come from the neighborhood to give back. It is fairly accurate to anticipate that one-third of those in attendance are hoping to serve; that requires good leadership so as not to be overwhelmed and become a negative experience for the volunteers and helpful neighbors. A leadership core that divides the tasks of each evening and oversees a portion of the volunteers makes for a more meaningful experience. Also, a four-plant approach is cheaper since they can all share vans and equipment. Beyond that, the camaraderie of planters working together at each other's churches makes for a supportive and encouraging mission environment. Further, a four-plant approach may have a positive impact on the way area churches step in to participate. Several suburban churches partnering to plant several urban churches at once is no small vision; it is large enough to stir congregations to sacrifice toward a big and serious impact on their nearby urban city.

Tom Sine reported that we have just crossed a threshold and become an urban planet, with more than 50 percent living in cities. That number will increase to 60 percent by 2020.[12] This is the time for the church of Jesus to create big plans for the cities, neighborhood by neighborhood.

Summation

In the New Testament, almost all of the stories occurred in the neighborhood.[13] Yet in today's church world, neighborhood visions are being under-considered. Trainer and consultant Alan Roxburgh believes that even many emergent churches are nothing more than new forms of inwardly focused churches that have little sense of their neighborhoods.[14] Why not go back to the neighborhood vision again? Identify a sore neighborhood; find a popular community room; start a dinner church; and then spread to another nearby challenged neighborhood, followed by another, until there is a thorough church presence in every high-density neighborhood in the city—this is a great vision. Perhaps one day there will be several dinner churches in every sore neighborhood in America.

7

FUNDING STREAMS

Financial Opportunities for Planting Dinner Churches

There are assumptions about church planting that do not translate to dinner churches. Dinner churches are organic social structures that assume incarnational approaches on the part of the planter, staff, and sites. The lower facility and program needs create an interesting budget. The average monthly costs for a dinner church are:

- Food: $1,200
- Personnel: $1,500
- Site rental: $400
  Total: $3,100

These costs assume that a church planter and team will augment their income with jobs located in the village, which is a part of incarnational living. These costs also assume that the churches are planted in clusters of four, so the planters from four dinner churches can converge to help each other with the needed leadership roles each site requires. Further, these costs assume that the team cooks the dinner. To cater the meals, add $1,400 per month to these costs; to have the caterer do the entrée only with the team doing the rest, add $600 per month to the costs. Lastly, these costs are based on the average of six sites that are located in the urban neighborhoods of Seattle. Community dinners not only vary by budget; they can also be funded by many more sources of income than a traditional church plant. This is due to its social-engagement focus. Following are a few insights and funding streams that a church planter should consider.

Tithe into Poverty

The tithe has been God's answer to poverty since the days of Moses, and a recurring theme throughout Scripture. The book of Deuteronomy makes it clear that a full third of the tithe was to be directed toward the poor and even referred to that portion as the "special tithe" or the "sacred gift" (see Deuteronomy 14:28–29; 26:12–13). The book of Acts demonstrates that the first-century church poured significant portions of their funds into the widows and orphans. In fact, the scriptural view of funding the poor reveals a lending relationship between God and the one who gives to the poor. Proverbs 19:17 says, "Whoever is generous to the poor lends to the LORD, and he will repay him for his deed" (ESV). The early church seemed to hold this lending view; even the poor gave to the poor because they expected the Lord to pay them back. A dinner church needs to restore the "tithe into poverty" understanding. Placing a bucket at the beginning of the buffet tables gives a way for every attender to grow in this area of partnering with Christ to lift the poor, even if they are poor. The widow in Mark 12:41–44, who was giving alms (that is, giving to charity), is the perfect example of how Christ applauds the poor when they lift the poor. The kingdom of God has always used common people to do great things. Tithing into poverty is an opportunity for even the "least of these" (Matthew 25:40) to be used in the kingdom. All members of the dinner church should be invited to participate in God's age-old plan for poverty.

Something beyond Nickels and Noses

Church plants, especially in sore neighborhoods, need to consider that a form of income beyond tithing is probably going to be needed.

Church leaders have been uncomfortable looking for funding beyond the tithing plan for fear that they are being unspiritual and outpacing God, but most church planters do not have the luxury of remaining exclusively tithe-centric. Pastor and best-selling author Mark Batterson observed that more than half of all church plants do not last one year.[1] The basic reason most do not make it is a lack of money. This is especially true in cities. While it may be wonderful that suburban leaders can make a church function from the discretionary income levels of suburban people, those who plant in challenged locations need to acknowledge that the same opportunities do not exist for them. Ed Stetzer stated that starting a church among the poor will have different cost factors than other planting assignments.[2] Urban settings are located on the most expensive land in the country. These costs translate down to every urban resident and every urban social structure. This poses a great challenge to all urban churches. Rick Rusaw said, "The great challenge of urban ministry in the U.S. is that the churches that are most in touch with the needs of the people often have the least ability and capacity to meet those needs. Most urban churches are stretched to the limit."[3] Urban and sore neighborhood costs are a financial fact that must be faced squarely; leaders need to admit that something beyond nickels and noses are needed.

Rent from Church Properties

Existing churches that are transforming into dinner churches may find that Christ is calling them to walk away from their facilities and into challenged neighborhoods altogether. While this is an emotional conversation, leaders need to remember that a building is just a tool, and it is not always the right tool for every mission. The dinner church, for example, is a vision that makes missionaries out of churchgoers and sends them into sore neighborhoods. That being said, there may come a time when a group senses that their facility is not located in a good walking village and is no longer a tool they can use. Ed Stetzer stated that if evangelicals are to be effective in reaching North American urban centers, they will actually need to abandon the thinking that ten acres of land and a brick building are essential to be successful.[4] Some groups that are transforming into mission-based churches may find it within themselves to leave their church campuses behind. Futurist and consultant Rex Miller predicted that many churches in the coming decade will shed their buildings in order to reinhabit their neighborhoods, turning to grassroots strategies to reach an emerging population with smaller-scale gatherings.[5]

It is likely that many churches will one day face the question, What do we do with our facilities now that they no longer fit our mission? Some groups might need to sell and reinvest their money. However, converting a church facility into rental property can create surprising levels of monthly income. The going price per foot to rent an improved education and business space is a dollar per foot on average. Thus, a twenty-thousand-square-foot church, which is average-sized, could bring a monthly income of $20,000. A lot of dinner churches can be planted for $20,000 a month. Montessori schools, child care schools, preschools, specialty schools for autism and the developmentally disabled, ethnic churches, and nonprofits are always looking for space to rent. I recommend that a good commercial agent be sought; even though their commissions are high, the net income they can produce for a church property will be more than worth it.

Schools and Financial Engines

Child care facilities, schools, and senior housing buildings have been used to augment church incomes for decades. While there is some risk, the dinner church, too, can find some healthy attachment with certain kinds of financial engines. Finding a funding engine for each dinner church is likely to be needed, so a prayerful search for different income streams is warranted. More and more mission-based churches are using schools, child cares, apartment buildings, coffee shops, drop-in centers, and cultural centers to give them inroads into their neighborhoods and help fund their apostolic expansion plans.

Financial Partners

Due to the obvious lift a community dinner church brings to the neighborhood, there are people who are desirous of helping struggling populations in underprivileged settings. While church leaders are not usually aware of this path, dinner church leaders need to anticipate businesses and individuals who are actively looking for ways to give back. For individual donors, there are several giving instruments available that allow them to take advantage of tax strategies and gain back a significant portion of their gift in tax-retained amounts. This is especially true of individuals earning more than 250,000 per year in their personal income. Consulting an experienced certified public accountant is recommended.

Partner Churches

No church planter should overlook the significant support of suburban churches. Forging relationships with nearby suburban churches that are interested in the needs of the city is indispensable. The planter needs this relationship for a thousand reasons, but the suburban church needs it too since their proclamation-based social construct makes it difficult to provide ways for people to engage in mission and practice the works of Christ. A partnership with a dinner church would provide a significant growth step for their people's Christlikeness. Philip Yancey wrote that suburban churches may have to look harder for mission opportunities and should consider a tie-in with an inner-city work.[6] Nearby churches have the need to find a place for mission expression, and a dinner church needs money and weekly missionaries to help them serve the gospel to rooms full of people with no church background. A partnership between a suburban church and a dinner church is a match made in heaven—literally.

Catamaran Churches

Some nearby suburban churches can take a greater role in a city-wide dinner church plant plan; they actually plant a dinner church themselves as a multisite gathering. The reason the "catamaran" designation is given to them is that they must be sophisticated enough to have two ministry natures, just as a catamaran boat has two hulls in the water. The proclamation-based church is a systems-oriented social construct; however, a dinner church is an organic-familial social construct. For a suburban church that wants to plant a dinner church, they will need to maintain a systems-orientation on Sunday mornings at their campus, but assume an organic-orientation at their dinner church site on a weeknight. If they do not take on a catamaran-like sophistication, their systematic methods will sicken their dinner church approach and limit its effectiveness. Still, some suburban churches are sophisticated enough to handle two different tools at different times in the week and should consider planting a dinner church in a sore neighborhood near them.

Some denominations have already forged partnership structures between existing churches and church planters. Some look to hand off the church to the planter in time; others keep the new plant and consider it another Sunday service, but in a different location. In the case of a dinner church, it is not only at a different location but also on a different night; yet it is still considered one of the weekend services of the main campus.

It is interesting to ponder the question, What are most churches planning to do to grow by one hundred people in attendance by this time next year? I would propose that most groups have no specific plan, and ought to consider the dinner church as partnership with an existing church.

The reasons a nearby suburban church should seriously consider planting a dinner church are: (1) most pastors feel an apostolic obligation to affect the sore neighborhoods that are near them, (2) it gives a Great Commission opportunity for their people to embrace a missionary identity and show up each week to practice the "works of Christ" spirituality, (3) existing staff can be re-tasked to move into the neighborhood and take on the pastoral role in the new location without interfering with their Sunday tasks, (4) there are probably some great cooks in the church that could form a culinary arts team to do the cooking in the church kitchen and transport the food in hot boxes to the dinner church site each week, and (5) with the personnel costs already covered by the church, a suburban church would only need to spend $2,000 a month to plant a dinner church. Most suburban churches could probably raise such a small amount, especially for such a large mission opportunity. A dinner church is a compelling vision—compelling enough to inspire monthly pledges from a congregation.

Grants

Again, due to the strong emphasis of lifting the marginalized populations, grants are available; however, these grants are not easy to get and usually require a professional grant writer. The Murdock Foundation, the Pew Foundation, and the Festus Stacy Foundation are all particularly interested in Christian groups getting involved in US poverty. Another avenue to consider is AmeriCorps, which provides yearlong volunteers with matching pay.

US Missions

Many denominations provide for US church planters to function as missionaries. This provides another potential stream of income for some dinner church planters.

Friends and Family

Cost of living is one of the reasons that most church-plant efforts fail, especially in the city. Thankfully, most church planters have a network of family members, previous churches, and friends who take a vested interest in the planter's efforts. Turning to these friends and family relationships for monthly pledge support is natural and can be achieved with simple phone calls. Planting a dinner church in a sore neighborhood is a compelling vision for people to invest in. These close relational circles usually add up to between $500 and $1,000 a month, helping augment the church planter's income.

Part-Time Jobs in the Neighborhood

Incarnational living is a nonnegotiable value for dinner church planters. Living within six blocks of their dinner church location so they can spend much time in the coffee shops and on the sidewalks of their neighborhood is worth fighting for. This opens up the possibility for a planter to find part-time work in the village that not only augments their income, but also augments their incarnational engagements, especially if the position has high visibility, such as a barista, waiter, or cashier. Of course, a spouse that works is also of great financial assistance for a church planter.

The Jesus Potluck

The agape feasts of the New Testament were potlucks that included the stranger and the poor around the tables of food prepared by Christians. Similarly, when John Wesley initiated his Stranger's Friend Society in London in the nineteenth century, he used the potluck approach to fill up their tables.[7] The early American church also understood the genius of the potluck to create a strong sense of family among their attenders. To do a potluck dinner church today would not only match a very rich Christian tradition, but it would also reduce the costs to merely the site rental. And that makes church planting affordable for many, many groups. I find it interesting that Jesus only challenged his disciples to pray to the Lord of the harvest to send workers, and not pray for money (Matthew 9:38). The early church did not seem to see financial hurdles in their church-planting efforts that we do today. That is because the only form of church planting was Jesus dinners that were offered potluck style, and that was not a very expensive proposition. We might do well to considered the Jesus potluck again.

Nothing but a Call

Church history is filled with pastors who went to a place with no money, contacts, team, or supporting churches. In fact, it was assumed that anyone graduating with a theology degree would be planting his or her own church, which meant feeling a call to a particular city or neighborhood, showing up with nothing but raw faith, trusting God to help raise enough money to afford the first month's rent of a storefront to begin Sunday services, and "carve that church out of the rock."[8] Most churches exist because someone birthed it through sacrifice, raw faith, and hard work. While that approach is almost impossible today with a traditional church-plant model, it is possible with the dinner church template. Some leaders might embrace the "carve it out of the rock" attitude, move into a neighborhood that stirs their souls, find supportive jobs, and trust God to help them raise the $1,800 monthly budget needed for food and site rental from people, businesses, nearby churches, tithes, and all other creative means as Christ leads them. The dinner churches of the future will all have many raw-faith stories to tell.

Summation

The church can no longer ignore sore neighborhoods because they cannot generate enough tithers to fund a traditional church plant; a new way of thinking is required. The church of Jesus must find it within itself to establish different funding streams. Scripturally, Christ's funding came from many sources. Some of them were surprising—prostitutes, tax collectors, and even the mouths of fish. In light of Jesus' funding plans, I would propose that we consider many different funding streams in this day, especially in the under-privileged areas where miracles are needed. Pastor and researcher Kennon Callahan said that money follows mission, not the other way around.[9] To revive the ancient agape feast is no small mission, especially if we consider planting a dinner church in every high-density neighborhood in the country. With such a compelling vision before us, let us keep our minds, our prayers, and our hands open for many funding streams to flow into the dinner church story.

CONCLUSION

So They Get to Go to Heaven Too...

At a critical time in the early church, John the Revelator repeated the refrain, "Anyone with ears to hear must listen to the Spirit and understand what he is saying to the churches" (Rev. 2:7, 11, 17, 29; 3:6, 13, 22). At the turn of that first century, the church needed to confront itself on issues. Today's church is in a similar moment; there are some things about our ways of doing church that need to be confronted. The declines in the American church are saying something loudly to us—if we have ears to hear it.

The Challenge: Unintended Elitism

Throughout US history, churches have predominantly located in middle- and upper-class neighborhoods, serving those who can afford the expensive proclamation-church model. This unintended elitism has left the church unable to imagine embracing the poor, and under-practiced in doing church in sore neighborhoods. All the while, most church leaders continue to assume that America is a middle-class nation. This is not true. Economic declines have persisted to the point that now, as mentioned previously, two out of five American families are relying on food banks.[1] In many of our towns, one out of three residents earn beneath the poverty line.[2] And the largest consumers of dog and cat food are senior citizens who cannot afford regular food.[3] The poor account for increasing portions of our American socioscape. It is this lower-third population where the greatest opportunity for the reviving of the American church exists—if we can confront our elitism and lift our eyes to observe this alarmingly large harvest.

The Opportunity: Sore Neighborhoods

Sore neighborhoods become visible because the residents who live there do not have the resources or the energy for groomed lawns and maintained houses. These sore locations are in every town, in varying degree, because the lower third must live somewhere. In my town, which is known as one of the wealthiest large cities in America, 30 percent earn below the poverty rate and another 30 percent live alone. Accordingly, when a neighborhood becomes predominantly populated by poor and isolated residents, its soreness becomes visible to even a casual missiologist. Leaders of the Christian mission should take notice of these locations. After all, there are more than twenty-three hundred Scriptures about lifting the poor.[4] The only topic more covered in the Bible is the theme of rescue and salvation. A simple study of the Gospels reveals that Christ spent much of his time with the poor people; that fact alone should inform the values of every church that is endeavoring to represent Christ well in their towns. Historically, the church's greatest relevance was garnered by the way they lifted the poor. Defining relevance as spiked hair, tattoos, and cool worship music needs to be replaced by a more primary relevance—churches helping their neighbors with serious issues, such as housing, food, clothes, jobs, and acceptance around a warm Christian table. Nothing will give a new church plant influence any faster than pursuing and lifting "the least of these" that live all around them (Matthew 25:40). The greatest missiological opportunity for the American church is not at most of our present addresses; it is in a sore neighborhood a few blocks away. This is even truer in urban settings. Jean Vanier predicted that a renaissance is coming; soon there will be a multitude of communities founded on adoration and presence for the poor, linked to the great communities of the church.

The Call: So They Get to Go to Heaven Too

Throughout church history, whenever Christ's people got serious about doing church for sore populations, they got serious about the dinner church. In fact, this was the manner of church that most defined the apostolic era, a clear scriptural point that was confirmed by key historians from the early centuries.[5] Dinner churches are so compelling to marginalized and isolated populations because they bring a feast, a family, and Jesus to a neighborhood in a very embracing way. What one experiences during an evening is: (1) a bountiful buffet table loaded with food, (2) an acoustic guitarist filling the room with worship songs, (3) a couple of artists painting pictures inspired from the Gospels, (4) linen-clad tables filled with neighbors from all walks of life eating together and becoming friends, and (5) a story about Christ and a prayer for favor at the end. Dinner churches fit the sociology of sore neighborhoods well.

After planting eight dinner churches in Seattle, the average attendance at the one-year point ranges between 80 and 280, in which one-third of the guests are financially challenged, another third are lonely and disconnected from any social group, and one-third are Christ-followers and Samaritans/humanitarians who have come to help lift their neighbors. The predictable success of the dinner church approach creates the possibility of a neighborhood-by-neighborhood expansion plan throughout a city.[6]

Identify a sore neighborhood, find a central community room, start a dinner church, and then consider spreading to another sore neighborhood. It is a situation where opportunity and simplicity meet; the opportunity of the sore neighborhood meets the simplicity of the dinner table church. To put an apostolic ear to the ground is to hear these challenged populations inviting us to be with them. And in this post-Christian day, for the church to be invited anywhere is no small thing. If these invitations are not modern versions of Macedonian calls, I don't know what is.

The American church has been doing proclamation-based churches in middle- and upper-class locations, especially since the 1960s. I propose it is time to start doing dinner churches in sore neighborhoods, so they can go to heaven too.

APPENDIX A

Seattle Training House

Community dinners in Seattle are not feeding programs or outreaches. They are dinner churches modeled after the agape feasts we read about in the New Testament. This is particularly important to the sore neighborhoods of America, and for the churches that are in need of a new sense of mission.

We believe that the Jesus dinner table theology provides an answer worthy of consideration for church leaders. The dinner church approach that is working so well from neighborhood to neighborhood in Seattle and other cities will work in numerous sore locations, and for the same reasons. We estimate there are thousands of sore neighborhoods across our nation; these are the places where dinner churches gain quick footing.

In 2011, we purchased a 1925 Craftsman home located a few blocks north of downtown to gather pastors and church planters for Seattle immersions that begin with observation and then move into training sessions. We are set up to offer church planters and plant teams a place to stay for a few nights, observe some dinner churches in action, and then engage in training conversations.

These visits include:

- accommodations at the training house (including a pool table, hot tub, location near the city zoo, and other nearby walking sites)
- light continental breakfasts each morning

- some free time during the day to enjoy Seattle
- opportunities to observe the dinner church sites in progress
- fireside training dialogues led by Verlon Fosner and the staff, along with coffee and dessert
- handbooks, articles, and other tools about the dinner church made available

To inquire about the dates of upcoming Seattle immersions, costs, daily schedules, transportation, or to get registration information, please go to our website: www.DinnerChurchCollective.net.

APPENDIX B

Thirteen Menu Options for Large Groups

Christians are known for being good cooks and using their food to build the kingdom of God. This reputation dates back to the days of Christ and the agape feasts; the dinner table was the perfect setting for the gospel to spread. It is in our spiritual DNA to serve up colorful, tasteful, and abundant feasts in the likeness of Christ.

We have three different dinner preparation arrangements: (1) fully catered meal, (2) hybrid prepared meal in which a caterer cooks the entrée and the staff cooks the remainder of the meal, or (3) the staff cooks the full meal. All three approaches work for different reasons at different sites. For instance, one site has a very poor kitchen, so we do the hybrid approach there. Another site is connected to the caterer's banquet room, so they cook that one. Another site has a great kitchen space and there is afternoon time available for the staff and culinary arts teams to prepare the complete meal.

All of our dinners are served from a buffet table with Sterno chafing dishes to keep them warm. Usually, three chafing dishes are needed, though there are a few menus that only need two.

Following are thirteen menus, which are enough dinner plans for one quarter, only needing to repeat a menu item four times in a year. Each of the following menus assumes that the ingredients will be purchased at a Cash & Carry or similar wholesale restaurant supplier. Further, each of the following menus is figured for one hundred portions, so divide or multiply the measurements accordingly.

MENUS

■ ■ ■ ■ ■ ■ ■ ■ ■ ■ ■ ▦ ▦ ▒ ░

Lasagna, Caesar Salad, Bread Sticks, Pepperoncini, Ice Cream

Ingredients:

6 frozen lasagnas (32 oz. each)
2 gallons spaghetti sauce
1 package of shredded mozzarella cheese (32 oz.)
1 tub of margarine (32 oz.)
garlic salt
garlic powder
100 sourdough bread sticks (or substitute equal amount of sour- dough bread)

4 packages of romaine lettuce (6 heads per package)
1 package of croutons (32 oz.)
2 bottles of Caesar salad dressing (32 oz. each)
1 package of shredded or shaved Parmesan cheese (16 oz.)
1 gallon of pepperoncini
1 gallon of sherbet (raspberry possibly)

Preparation:

1. Preheat the oven to 400 degrees. Remove frozen lasagnas from their tin containers, and place them two at a time in a full-size baking pan. Pour all the spaghetti sauce equally over the frozen lasagna in the three pans. Cover with a foil lid and put all three pans in the oven. Bake for 3 hours, or until interior temperature reaches 140 degrees. Remove the foil lid and sprinkle the entire package of mozzarella cheese equally over the three pans. Bake uncovered for another half hour, or until cheese is melted and turning a light, golden brown. (Allow 3.5 hours total for cooking this dish.)

2. Melt large amounts of butter in a large frying pan on the stovetop. Stir in generous doses of garlic salt and garlic powder. Lightly fry the bread sticks (or sliced-up sourdough bread) until lightly brown. Put in warmer until served.

3. Slice all of the romaine in a large salad bowl, add the package of croutons, and then stir in all the Caesar salad dressing. Mix well; garnish with shaved Parmesan. (Note: for freshness' sake, don't prepare the salad until a few minutes before serving.)
4. Place the pepperoncini in a bowl.
5. Serve the sherbet into small serving cups.

■ ■ ■ ■ ■ ■ ■ ■ ■ ■ ■ ■ ▪ ▪ ▫

Chicken-Fried Steak, Instant Mashed Potatoes, Country Gravy, Ranch Salad, Corn, Rolls, Brownies

Ingredients:

40 lbs. of frozen chicken-fried steak (breaded)

1 bottle of vegetable oil (32 oz.)

½ gallon of whole milk

2 packages of instant mashed potatoes (80 servings per package)

1 tub of margarine (32 oz.)

1 tub of sour cream (32 oz.)

2 packages of country gravy (makes 1 gallon each)

4 gallons of whole-kernel corn

4 packages of mixed greens

3 cucumbers

1 package of cherry tomatoes

1 small package of cheddar cheese

1 package of croutons (32 oz.)

2 bottles of ranch dressing (32 oz. each)

100 dinner rolls

100 servings of large cooked/frosted brownies

Preparation:

1. Fry the breaded chicken-fried steaks in vegetable oil in frying pans on stovetop until golden brown. Place in rows in three large baking pans and put in warmer.
2. Boil water and add milk according to instructions on instant mashed potato package; mix the potatoes into the water/milk; add in generous amounts of margarine and sour cream. Lightly salt while mixing. Place in three baking pans and put in warmer.
3. Prepare the gravy according to the package directions. Pour into a baking pan and put in warmer.

4. Boil water, add all corn, and stir in generous amounts of butter; lightly salt. Place in baking pan and put on warmer.

5. Place mixed greens, sliced cucumbers, cherry tomatoes, cheddar cheese, and croutons together with ranch dressing. Add a top dusting of croutons, cheddar cheese, and tomatoes for presentation. (For freshness' sake, prepare salad just minutes before serving.)

6. Serve rolls in a large bowl, with margarine spooned into a bowl and an accompanying butter knife.

7. Slice the brownies in one-inch-by-one-inch pieces.

■ ■ ■ ■ ■ ■ ■ ■ ■ ■ ■ ▪ ▪ ░ ░

Pulled Pork Sandwiches, Coleslaw, Baked Beans, Chips, Cookies

Ingredients:

6 shredded, pulled pork packages
   (5 lbs. each)
4 gallons of canned baked beans
100 hamburger buns
4 packages of coleslaw mix

64 oz. of coleslaw dressing
6 large, family-sized bags of potato
   chips
100 cookies

Preparation:

1. Preheat the oven to 350 degrees. Place the shredded pork in three baking pans (two packages in each), and bake for 2 hours.

2. Warm four gallons of baked beans in a large pot on the stovetop, and pour into a baking pan.

3. Place the buns in a baking pan; put in chafer early to warm.

4. Combine coleslaw mix with dressing, and serve in large bowl.

5. Serve chips in a large bowl.

6. Serve cookies on a large platter.

Dijon Chicken, Scalloped Potatoes, Carrots, Raspberry/Bleu Cheese Salad, Rolls, Brownies

Ingredients:

40 lbs. of frozen chicken pieces

32 oz. honey Dijon mustard

120 servings of instant scalloped potatoes

milk and butter for scalloped potatoes

4 gallons of canned carrots

1 cup butter (for carrots)

4 packages of mixed greens

1 package of bleu cheese crumbles (32 oz.)

1 package of candied pecans (16 oz.)

1 package of fresh raspberries

2 bottles raspberry salad dressing (32 oz. each)

100 dinner rolls

1 tub of margarine

100 servings of frosted brownies

Preparation:

1. Preheat the oven to 350 degrees. Place chicken pieces in a baking pan and bake until the interior temperature reaches 130 degrees; smear a thick layer of honey Dijon mustard across the top and continue cooking to 160 degrees.
2. Cook scalloped potatoes according to package instructions, adding milk and butter as needed.
3. Place the carrots in a large pot on the stove and add water until covered. Add in one cup of butter, and warm.
4. Place the greens in a large bowl. Stir in the bleu cheese crumbles, candied pecans, and fresh raspberries. Stir in the raspberry dressing. Garnish with a sprinkling of bleu cheese crumbles, pecans, and raspberries.
5. Serve rolls in a large bowl, with the tub of margarine spooned into a bowl and an accompanying butter knife.
6. Cut brownies in one-inch-by-one-inch squares.

Meatloaf, Instant Mashed Potatoes, Brown Gravy, Balsamic Salad, Carrots, Rolls, Cake

Ingredients:

15 lbs. of ground beef
15 lbs. of ground pork
6 onions, finely chopped
1 large bag of oyster crackers
18 eggs
½ cup of soy sauce
½ cup of Worcestershire sauce
3 cups of shredded carrots
Black pepper to taste
1 bottle of ketchup
4 gallons of canned carrots
2 tubs of margarine

1 package brown sugar (16 oz.)
120 servings of instant mashed potatoes
2 cucumbers
2 packs of brown gravy
4 packs of mixed greens
1 pack of cherry tomatoes
2 packs of croutons
2 bottles balsamic salad dressing (32 oz. each)
100 dinner rolls
100 servings of sheet cake

Preparation:

1. Preheat the oven to 350 degrees. Mix ground beef, ground pork, onions, oyster crackers, eggs, soy sauce, Worcestershire sauce, carrots, and black pepper in a large bowl. Form into a stand-alone loaves and place in a baking pan. Spread ketchup over the top of the loaves. (Note: leave an inch between loaves if more than one is placed in the pan.) Bake until the internal food temperature reaches 160 degrees.

2. Pour four cans of carrots into a large pot. Drain off water so as to only cover to the top of the carrots. Add a half cup of margarine and some brown sugar, warm, and pour into a pan.

3. Prepare the instant potatoes according to the package directions. (Note: only prepare one box at a time.)

4. Slice the cucumbers. Mix the greens, cucumbers, tomatoes, and croutons with the balsamic dressing. Garnish with a top sprinkle of tomatoes and croutons. Serve in a large salad bowl.

5. Serve rolls in a large bowl, and spoon the entire tub of margarine into a serving bowl, and set a butter knife alongside.
6. Slice cake in one-inch-by-one-inch pieces and serve on a platter.

■　■　■　■　■　■　■　■　■　▪　▫　▫　▫

Soft Tortilla Tacos, Toppings, Black Beans, Chips, Salsa Bar, Cookies

Ingredients:

30 lbs. of ground hamburger meat
2 cups of taco seasoning
100 large flour tortillas
4 gallon cans of black beans
1 large bunch/bag of cilantro, divided
1 small box of tomatoes
4 large bunches of green onions
1 large bag of shredded lettuce
1 bag of shredded cheddar cheese (32 oz.)

1 bag of shredded mozzarella cheese (32 oz.)
1 quart-sized tub of sour cream
1 gallon can of red salsa
1 gallon can of green salsa
1 gallon can of any other kind of salsa
164 oz. of tortilla chips
100 cookies

Preparation:

1. Fry the ground hamburger. Mix in the taco seasoning to taste.
2. Place the flour tortillas in a baking pan and warm in oven or for over an hour in a chafer.
3. Warm the four cans of black beans in a large pot on the stovetop. Pour into a baking pan; garnish with cut cilantro pieces.
4. Cut up the tomatoes and onions and put in bowls. Mix the lettuce and chopped cilantro in another bowl. Place both cheeses in bowls. Spoon sour cream in a separate bowl.
5. Place the three salsas in three separate bowls.
6. Place chips in a large bowl.
7. Place cookies on a platter.

■ ■ ■ ■ ■ ■ ■ ■ ■ ▪ ▪ ▪ ▫ ▫

Baked Chicken in Sweet Baby Ray's Sauce, Instant Mashed Potatoes, BBQ Brown Gravy, Green Beans, Balsamic Salad, Sliced Bread, Lemon Bars

Ingredients:

40 lbs of chicken legs, wings, and thighs

1 large container of Sweet Baby Ray's sauce

Pepper to taste

1 gallon of whole milk

1 tub of margarine

2 boxes of instant mashed potatoes

2 packs of brown gravy to make two gallons

4 gallons of canned green beans

1 package of sliced almonds (32 oz.), divided

4 packages of mixed greens

1 pack of cherry tomatoes

1 package of croutons (32 oz.)

2 bottles of balsamic dressing (32 oz. each)

100 dinner rolls

100 servings of lemon bars

Preparation:

1. Preheat the oven to 375 degrees and bake the chicken in baking pans until internal temperature reaches 150 degrees. Then pour and brush Sweet Baby Ray's sauce generously over the chicken, and continue baking until interior temperature reaches 165 degrees. Garnish with pepper.

2. Heat water, milk, and butter and mix with instant mashed potatoes according to the instructions on the box. Put in a pan; garnish with some small chunks of butter melting on the top.

3. Prepare the gravy according to the instructions on the gravy packet.

4. Warm up the green beans on a pot on the stovetop. Place in a pan; garnish with sliced almonds and pepper.

5. Mix the greens, tomatoes, sliced almonds, and croutons together with the balsamic dressing.

6. Serve rolls in a large bowl, with tub of margarine spooned into a bowl and an accompanying butter knife.

7. Cut up the lemon bars in one-inch-by-one-inch squares.

Pork Loin, Rice, Orange Sauce, Ranch Salad, Green Beans, Rolls, Bundt Cake

Ingredients:

30 lbs. of pork loin

salt and pepper

1 bag of rice (5 lbs.)

4 large jars of orange marmalade (16 oz. each)

3 tablespoons of crushed red pepper

4 gallons of canned green beans

1 large package of sliced almonds, divided

4 large packages of mixed greens

2 large packages of green onions

1 large package of cherry tomatoes

2 bottles of ranch dressing (32 oz. each)

2 packages of croutons

100 dinner rolls

1 tub of margarine

100 servings of Bundt cake

Preparation:

1. Place whole pork loin chunks in three baking pans. Generously salt and pepper the top. Bake in oven at 350 degrees until internal temperature reaches 145 degrees.
2. Cook the rice in a rice cooker.
3. Mix the orange marmalade, three tablespoons of crushed red pepper, and one cup of pork loin drippings. Warm in a saucepan.
4. Cook rice in a rice cooker. (Serve by ladling the gravy over the pork and rice a plate at a time at the buffet table.)
5. Pour four cans of green beans into a large pot, and add water to cover. Warm, place in a baking pan, and garnish with sliced almonds.
6. Mix greens, chopped green onions, croutons, and tomatoes with the ranch dressing. Garnish with croutons and sliced almonds.
7. Serve rolls in a large bowl, with tub of margarine spooned into a bowl and an accompanying butter knife.
8. Slice the Bundt cake into thin pieces.

■ ■ ■ ■ ■ ■ ■ ■ ■ ▦ ▦ ▦ ▦ ▦ ▦

Sausage and Roasted Tomatoes Penne Pasta, Caesar Salad, Sourdough Bread, Kalamata Olives, Ice Cream

Ingredients:

20 lbs. of ground Italian sausage

120 servings of penne pasta

1 gallon of heavy cream

3 gallons of diced Italian tomatoes

parsley, for garnish

4 packages of romaine lettuce (6 heads per package)

1 package of croutons (32 oz.)

2 bottles of Caesar dressing (32 oz. each)

1 package of shredded or shaved Parmesan cheese (32 oz.)

100 servings of sourdough bread

1 tub margarine (32 oz.)

1 container of Kalamata olives (64 oz.)

1 gallon of ice cream

Preparation:

1. Fry the Italian sausage in large frying pans on the stovetop; drain off the grease. Cook the penne pasta in a large pot according to the package directions. Pour in the sausage, heavy cream, and diced Italian tomatoes, and warm to satisfaction. Pour into a baking pan, garnish with green parsley and Parmesan cheese.

2. Slice up all of the romaine lettuce, add the package of croutons, and then stir in the Caesar dressing. Mix well and garnish with shaved Parmesan. (Note: for freshness' sake, don't prepare the salad until a few minutes before serving.)

3. Slice up the sourdough loaves in one-inch widths. Serve in a large bowl, next to a bowl of margarine accompanied by a butter knife.

4. Serve Kalamata olives in a large bowl.

5. Serve ice cream in small bowls.

Fried Chicken, Instant Mashed Potatoes, Country Gravy, Bleu Cheese Salad, Carrots, Rolls, Brownies

Ingredients:

50 lbs. of chicken legs, wings, thighs

2 bottles vegetable oil (32 oz. each)

salt and pepper

parsley flakes, for garnish

120 servings of instant mashed potatoes

½ gallon of whole milk

2 tubs of butter or margarine (32 oz. each)

1 tub of sour cream (32 oz.)

2 packs of country gravy (makes 1 gallon each)

4 gallons of canned sliced carrots

1 package of brown sugar (16 oz.)

4 large packs of mixed greens

1 package of bleu cheese chunks (32 oz.)

1 package of candied pecans (32 oz.)

2 bottles of bleu cheese salad dressing (32 oz. each)

100 dinner rolls

100 servings of brownies

Preparation:

1. Fry the chicken in vegetable oil in large frying pans on the stovetop. Place in baking pan and garnish with salt, pepper, and parsley flakes.
2. Prepare instant mashed potatoes according to instructions on the box, adding milk as needed, and then stir in butter and sour cream. Salt to taste. Pour into baking pan.
3. Boil water and mix in gravy according to instructions on packet. Salt and pepper to taste.
4. Warm up carrots in a large pot on the stovetop. Stir in butter and brown sugar to taste. Pour into a baking pan.
5. Mix greens, bleu cheese chunks, and candied pecans with the bleu cheese dressing, and garnish with a dusting of pecans and additional bleu cheese chunks.
6. Serve rolls in a large bowl, with a tub of margarine spooned into a bowl and an accompanying butter knife.
7. Cut brownies in one-inch-by-one-inch squares.

■ ■ ■ ■ ■ ■ ■ ■ ▥ ▦ ▦ ▧ ▨ ░ ░

Ham in Apple Juice, Instant Scalloped Potatoes, Green Beans and Almonds, Raspberry Pecan Salad, Sliced Bread, Lemon Bars

Ingredients:

40 lbs. of boneless cooked ham

4 large containers of apple juice concentrate

Black pepper

120 servings of instant scalloped potatoes

1 tub of margarine (32 oz.)

1 gallon of whole milk

4 gallons of green beans (or same amount of frozen green beans)

1 package of sliced almonds (32 oz.)

4 packs of mixed greens

1 package of candied pecans (32 oz.)

1 large pack of fresh strawberries

2 bottles of raspberry salad dressing (32 oz. each)

1 small package of Gorgonzola cheese chunks (16 oz.)

100 servings of bread loaves

100 servings of lemon bars

Preparation:

1. Preheat the oven to 350 degrees.
2. Slice ham in half lengthwise. Place cut side down in baking pan. Pour apple juice concentrate at the rate of one container per ten pounds of ham. Pepper the top. Bake in oven until internal temperature reaches 130 degrees. Splash the apple juice on the top and give a fresh dusting of pepper before serving.
3. Bake the scalloped potatoes according to the instructions on the box, adding margarine and milk as needed.
4. Warm the green beans in a large pot on the stovetop. Drain the water, pour the green beans into a baking pan, stir in margarine and sliced almonds, and garnish with additional sliced almonds and pepper.
5. Mix the greens, pecans, and sliced strawberries with the raspberry salad dressing, and garnish with the Gorgonzola cheese chunks.
6. Slice the bread loaves into one-inch widths and serve with a bowl of margarine and an accompanying butter knife.
7. Cut the lemon bars in one-inch-by-inch squares.

Spaghetti in Meat Sauce, Caesar Salad, Garlic Bread, Brownies

Ingredients:

20 lbs. of ground beef
4 gallons of spaghetti sauce
fresh parsley, for garnish
120 servings of spaghetti noodles
1 tub of margarine (32 oz.)
garlic salt
garlic powder
100 inches of sourdough bread in
  loaf form

4 packages romaine lettuce (6 heads
  per package)
1 package of croutons (32 oz.)
2 bottles of Caesar salad dressing
  (32 oz. each)
1 package of shredded or shaved
  Parmesan cheese (32 oz.)
100 servings of frosted brownies

Preparation:

1. Fry the ground beef in frying pans and drain off the grease. Mix into a large pot with spaghetti sauce and warm to satisfaction. Pour into baking pan and garnish with parsley.
2. Boil water and cook spaghetti to desired softness. Drain water; add a half cup of butter or margarine. Place noodles in a baking pan.
3. Melt large amounts of butter or margarine in a large frying pan on the stovetop. Stir in generous doses of garlic salt and garlic powder. Cut the sourdough loaves in one-inch widths, and fry both sides until lightly brown. Put in a baking pan.
4. Slice up all the packages of romaine, add the package of croutons, and then stir in the Caesar dressing. Mix well, and garnish with shaved Parmesan. (Note: for freshness' sake, don't prepare the salad until a few minutes before serving.)
5. Cut brownies in one-by-one-inch squares.

Baked Brisket, Baked Red Potatoes, Au Jus Sauce, Mild Horseradish Sauce, Corn, Honey Mustard Salad, Rolls, Cake

Ingredients:

40 lbs. of beef brisket
salt and pepper
40 lbs. of red potatoes
2 tubs of margarine (32 oz.)
1 gallon of au jus sauce
64 oz. of mild horseradish sauce
4 gallons of canned whole kernel corn
4 packages of mixed greens

3 cucumbers
1 package of grape tomatoes
1 package of croutons (32 oz.)
2 bottles of honey mustard salad
    dressing (32 oz. each)
100 dinner rolls
100 servings of sheet cake

Preparation:

1. Preheat the oven to 375 degrees. Place brisket in baking pans, salt and pepper, and bake until internal temperature reaches 145 degrees.
2. Halve the red potatoes, spread out one layer deep in baking pans, brush on a light coating of melted butter or margarine, and bake at 375 degrees until golden brown. Salt and pepper.
3. Warm au jus sauce on the stove.
4. Pour horseradish sauce into a large bowl.
5. Warm the corn on the stovetop and place in a chafer to keep warm.
6. Mix greens, sliced cucumbers, grape tomatoes, and croutons with honey mustard salad dressing. Garnish with additional croutons.
7. Serve rolls with a tub of margarine spooned into a bowl and an accompanying butter knife.
8. Cut sheet cake into one-inch-by-one-inch squares.

Summation

While these menus are commonly used, many of the culinary teams do their shopping at Cash & Carry (a restaurant supply warehouse) and put off forming the menu until they see what is on sale and what is available that day. Selecting the meat or entrée, then choosing a starch, followed by a vegetable, a matching salad, a dessert, and throwing in a few bags of dinner rolls is actually easier to do on the spot than what many imagine. It is possible to shadow one of the community dinner's culinary teams through a buying trip and a complete meal-prep experience upon request.

Often, we are asked if people with few food skills can learn to do this. Our answer is yes, a thousand times yes! The future belongs to the bold! That pertains to many things associated with the dinner church, including the kitchen. God will help a couple or team find their way.

APPENDIX C

A Security Plan for Dinner Church Gatherings

The big and welcoming nature of community dinners brings in all kinds of people. After one year of social balancing, most sites develop into a neighborhood family in which one-third are financially challenged, one-third are suffering from isolation, and one-third are the good Samaritans who have shown up to help. Security events are rare in most neighborhoods, but a team should always be responsibly prepared for a security event. Most of the time this familial structure self-monitors. However, there are a few individuals who do not work well with social structures and need additional assistance to help them maintain the peace of the dinner room. The following security plan exists to aid in these kinds of situations.

Security Risks

Following are seven security concerns that can threaten a dinner church:

- Intoxication
- Verbal abuse (including hate speech)
- Potential threat of physical abuse
- Visible presence of drugs/alcohol/weapons
- Verbal sexual harassment
- Theft
- Mental instability

While it is recommended that security personnel be trained and appointed to serve at every site, each community dinner lead team needs to have a precise understanding of these seven risks, have an eye for the small beginnings of these infractions, and understand the point at which a security response is required. Working as a team of leaders with the security personnel always produces the best results; security is a team effort.

Security Responses

To have a thorough understanding of the seven security risks enables an understanding of the appropriate response to each event. This policy approach to security allows for adequate training of the leaders and enables all leaders to know how to help during a security event. Again, security risks are rare for most neighborhoods, but they do occur occasionally and warrant a measure of preparation.

A security response is a behavior that is employed by the security team and leaders that prevents a security risk from disturbing the peace of a dinner church in progress. Following are ten security actions/responses that a dinner team must know, be trained in, and be prepared to employ:

- **Eyes On**—This is the action of watching a person who is a potential risk in a way that makes the individual aware that he or she is being watched. This creates presence and accountability; it is passive in nature but it eliminates most threats.
- **Blocking**—This is the action of stepping in front of someone who has obviously been drinking or appears irritable to measure his or her suitability to be in a dinner room. This practice is usually only employed by the security person working the front door. If the person gets frustrated at the blocker, then he or she is judged unsuitable to enter the dinner site. If the individual steps back peacefully and passively, then he or she is usually given access.
- **9-1-1**—This is the action of texting "9-1-1" on a cell phone to other on-site security personnel and leaders so as to create strength in numbers during a security event. Simply having the other

personnel on speed dial and texting "9-1-1" is both easy and a commonly understood signal for quick response.

- **Distracting Conversation**—This is the action of measuring a brewing conflict and distracting the key participants by engaging them in a different subject. This works exceptionally well with intoxicated people, but has a positive effect on most people. Sometimes, God provides humor and something that engages everyone in laughter at this point; laughter is a divine thing that restores social order faster than anything else.
- **Defusing Conversation**—This is the action of calmly calling out a person, to protect the peace of the room, pulling him aside to talk over his conflict with a leader rather than the person with whom he is frustrated, or leading someone to sit at a different table. The wise use of distance defuses many conflicts.
- **Herding**—This is the action of several security personnel and leaders calmly walking someone to the door while maintaining personal space distance. This works exceptionally well on an intoxicated person. It is also probably required once a volatile person has been disinvited from inside the room.
- **Warning**—This is the action of recognizing that someone is right on the edge of a risk behavior and calmly instructing him that if he continues, he will be disinvited. This should be done sparsely, as a community dinner does not want to get the reputation of frequently "kicking people out." However, a line does exist that, once crossed, must result in someone being removed for not protecting the peace of the room. In many situations, the knowledge that such a line exists causes troublemakers to quiet down. Warning should be done carefully. In the event of a very emotional situation between attenders, a mean drunk, or mental instability, it can actually inflame the situation. Those three situations respond best to herding.
- **Hand-off**—This is the action of one security person asking another security person or leader to deal with someone who is unusually frustrating. This is an important action to keep the security personnel from crossing a line in their security responses with

someone. There are those who love to create conflict and will needle a security person until he or she reacts wrongly. When the frustration is rising, pull out the 9-1-1 response and get another leader dealing with the offender.

- **Disinvite**—This is the action of instructing someone that he or she is not allowed to attend the dinner or that he or she must leave the dinner. This is usually only done by the lead security person and is better implemented at the front door rather than inside the room. To place the lead security person at the front door, employing disinvites at the door, solves more challenging disinvites later inside the room. All disinvites are softened by offering food-to-go on the sidewalk.

- **Call Police**—This action is taken when a security event has become more physical than the security personnel is authorized to act on. If someone brandishes a weapon, physically attacks a security person, or attacks another guest, it is time to get the police involved. This should be a last resort. To have the police showing up week after week at a dinner site would have a very negative effect on the "bringing neighbors together" goal of community dinners. Also, there is a physical nature of the sidewalks; they often lend themselves to physical altercations but good neighbors can gently and skillfully separate people who are fighting, without involving the law. While it does warrant a disinvite of the people involved, most things do not require police action. In the years we have been doing dinner churches in Seattle, we have only had to call the police a few times.

Understanding the security response terminology is profoundly important for a lead team. The appropriate security response to employ for a particular security risk is usually quite obvious; however, following is a grid of the recommended responses to the seven security risks:

Security Risk	Responses
Intoxication:	**Eyes On Blocking/Disinvite**
	<ul><li>Determination made by security whether an individual is fall-down drunk or aggressive drunk.</li><li>Step in front of the individual to determine response.</li><li>If they fail to remain civil during the blocking technique imposed by the security personnel, they are not allowed in the room.</li><li>A plate of food is offered on the sidewalk.</li><li>If someone has been drinking but is not fall-down drunk or aggressive, he or she is allowed to stay.</li></ul>
Verbal Abuse	**Distraction/Diffusing Conversation**
	<ul><li>This includes escalating volume, foul language, or insults.</li><li>If this happens, it is usually in a food line over someone cutting in line.</li><li>Any leader who is walking amid the folks can step in and distract/defuse.</li></ul>
Potential Threat of Physical Abuse	**Disinvite/Herding/Police**
	<ul><li>Pushing between guests warrants a 9-1-1 text to lead security, and both parties are disinvited.</li><li>Anyone brandishing weapons warrants a 9-1-1 to lead security and a disinvite.</li><li>Herding is almost always needed at this point to get the risk out of the room.</li><li>Note: community dinners security authority is mostly observation-oriented. Physical constraint is in the purview of the police department of any city. The only exception is if another person is in immediate danger.</li></ul>
Visible Drugs/Alcohol/ Weapons	**Warning/Disinvite**
	<ul><li>Kindly ask the individual to remove contraband from the room. If medically necessary (such as medical marijuana), it must be kept out of sight.</li></ul>

Verbal Sexual Harassment	Distraction/Warning/Disinvite
	▪ Distraction conversation curbs inappropriate sexual talk quite well. ▪ Mild infraction receives one warning. ▪ Major infraction results in a disinvite.
Theft	**Eyes On**
	▪ Eyes On reduces the opportunity and is usually all that is needed. ▪ Remove the opportunity: iPods, purses, etc. ▪ Do not go into investigation mode. ▪ Advise the individual not to confront a suspect in the dinner room, but to contact the police. ▪ Always notify lead security of such a conversation.
Mental Instability	**Soft Contact**
	▪ Instructions for dealing with a mentally unstable person are the same as for all the previous situations, but with special understanding for the individual's mental state. ▪ Determine whether mentally unstable individuals are a threat to others or themselves. ▪ If a response is required, soft contact, non-provoking tones, and nonthreatening postures often help; even so, expect the unpredictable.

Key Considerations

There are a few things associated with proximities and interactions between security personnel and leaders that heighten the security of a dinner site. First, the lead security person always works the front door. This cuts down on people who have been formerly disinvited getting into the room. This should always be the most trained individual and the one with the most security authority. Having one person in charge keeping individuals who are risky in mind is important for managing risk from week to week.

Second, have one security person stationed inside employing Eyes On over the whole room. This cuts down on many difficulties.

Third, security personnel might consider using earbuds. This is both helpful for 9-1-1 texts, but also establishes a passive sense of authority for all the guests to know who is keeping the peace. It also helps establish a sense of identity for the volunteers that have been trained in the security policy to feel they are filling an important role. Because security events happen so seldom, it is easy to think that the security role is unimportant; however, once a security event occurs, its importance becomes clear.

Fourth, regular eye contact between security personnel and leaders is an ongoing nonverbal communication of potential-risk individuals. Oftentimes, a security volunteer can "eye-locate" a person and communicate to a leader who to go sit by and minister to. Also, a leader can direct a security personnel with their glance to employ Eyes On action and increase a sense of presence to a certain conversation, table, or individual. An ounce of prevention is truly worth a pound of cure when it comes to dinner-room security.

Fifth, when a leader or security person is at his or her emotional limit, it is better to turn an irritating individual over to another leader than to raise one's voice and demonstrate something beneath our familial value.

Sixth, if there are gangs in the neighborhood, this requires a threat assessment from the local police gang enforcement office before beginning the community dinner.

Each brings a different approach and set of considerations.

Service Animals

From time to time guests want to bring their dogs into the meal site. This creates difficulties for many people who worry about cleanliness. Due to the close proximity to food, and health department suggestions, we only allow certified service animals into the meal sites. However, we are willing to serve anyone on the sidewalk that has a noncertified animal. Since service animal vests can be purchased online, our security personnel require the actual certification for proof. If for some reason the person does not have it with him or her, but states that the animal is a certified service animal, then the front-door personnel must evaluate the grooming and the attentive stance of the animal, both of which demonstrate professional training. If the grooming and attentive stance are obvious, the individual and service animal are given entry.

Summation

Community dinners are called to lift broken people, just as our Master did when he was on earth. It serves us well to be aware of how frustrating life is for broken people. That frustration radiates toward anyone who will listen. Often, a community dinner offers the only ear that will listen. Community dinners wrap themselves in grace, favor, and courage, and embrace people that sanitized America would rather ignore. That embrace is a holy calling, one that requires wisdom and a common-sense security plan. The best form of security is the kind that deals with things in their infancy, when responses and actions are not even noticed by the guests. However, if a risk presents itself, a security team that is trained in appropriate security actions and coordinated in their response restores the greatest sense of peace to the room. It is our faith that if we prepare ourselves, we can expect Christ to be a ring of fire around our efforts. After all, we have said yes to his call to be his presence in the sore neighborhoods of America.

APPENDIX D

A Dinner Church Planting Checklist

When the apostle Paul went to Thessalonica, he was able to start an agape dinner church, train a pastor, and appoint elders in only three months.[1] We have found a similar timetable in our Seattle dinner churches; three months' lead time is usually all that is needed. The following checklist assumes a short time period, and has been prepared by a cooperative effort of the pastors of the Seattle and Denver dinner churches.

Site Selection

❏ Identify sore neighborhoods

❏ Do sidewalk observations during potential evening dinner gatherings with team

❏ Listen for which neighborhood is calling you (Macedonian-type call)

❏ After a neighborhood chooses you, locate their common community room

❏ Establish a relationship and rental contract with the community space

Promotion

- ❏ Establish/raise the start-up and monthly budget from churches, friends, and family
- ❏ Design and construct A-frame signs
- ❏ Create tabletop A-frame signs (reference to Christ story)
- ❏ Display posters in area businesses and coffee shops
- ❏ Hand out flyers with menus
- ❏ Network with local businesses

Missionaries/Volunteers

- ❏ Look for churches to provide teams to set up, serve, do worship music sets, and, the largest role in the house, sit with guests and turn strangers into family
- ❏ Share vision with pastors to establish church partnerships
- ❏ Share vision with small groups to enlist missionaries (Christians looking to serve)
- ❏ Advertise on local college post boards for artists and musicians (possible jazz night, etc.)
- ❏ Vision meetings with plant team/missionaries/Samaritans/etc.
- ❏ Enlist head cook and culinary team
- ❏ Enlist musicians, artists, sidewalk pastor (security), and buffet table leader

Equipment

- ❏ Cargo vehicle
- ❏ Sound equipment
- ❏ Artists easels and hardboard to paint on (cheaper than canvas options)
- ❏ Tables and chairs (hopefully provided by the rental site)

Food/Food Supplies

- ❏ Hot boxes
- ❏ Coffeepots
- ❏ Salt and pepper
- ❏ Sugar/creamer
- ❏ Water pitchers
- ❏ Sterno chafing dishes
- ❏ Serving bowls
- ❏ Paper plates/cups
- ❏ Plastic cutlery sets with napkins
- ❏ Table linens with laundry bags

Worship/Music/Artists

- ❏ Develop evening schedule (serving, musicians, Christ story, line closed, etc.)
- ❏ Create worshipful playlist for background music when there are no musicians
- ❏ Go to work turning strangers into friends, friends into Christ-followers, and Christ-followers into missionaries

NOTES

Introduction

1. James Emery White, *Rethinking the Church: A Challenge to Creative Redesign in an Age of Transition* (Grand Rapids, MI: Baker Books, 2003), 20.
2. Ed Stetzer, *Planting New Churches in a Postmodern Age* (Nashville, TN: Broadman & Holman Publishers, 2003), 10.
3. Jim Cymbala, "It Is Time to Change Something" (lecture, Orlando, FL, August 6, 2013).
4. David Olson, *12 Surprising Facts about the American Church* (American Church Research Project, 2008), PowerPoint presentation, 38 frames, available at http://www.theamericanchurch.org.
5. Stetzer, *Planting New Churches in a Postmodern Age*, 10.
6. Alton Garrison, *Hope in America's Crisis* (Springfield, MO: Gospel Publishing House, 2007), 34.
7. Alan R. Johnson, *Apostolic Function in 21st Century Missions* (Pasadena, CA: William Carey Library, 2009), 22.
8. Tom Sine, *The New Conspirators: Creating the Future One Mustard Seed at a Time* (Downers Grove, IL: InterVarsity Press, 2008), 178–80.

Chapter 1: The Historic Dinner Church

1. Christine D. Pohl, *Making Room: Recovering Hospitality as a Christian Tradition* (Grand Rapids, MI: W. B. Eerdmans Publishing Co., 1999), 3.
2. Robert Stallman, "Divine Hospitality in the Pentateuch" (PhD diss., University of Michigan, 1999), 184.
3. Ibid., 182.
4. Ibid., 233.
5. Ibid., 272.
6. Ibid., 217.
7. Ibid., 128.
8. John M. Perry, *Exploring the Evolution of the Lord's Supper in the New Testament*, Exploring Scripture Series (Kansas City, MO: Sheed & Ward, 1994), 4.

9. Stallman, "Divine Hospitality in the Pentateuch," 243.
10. Perry, *Exploring the Evolution of the Lord's Supper in the New Testament*, vi.
11. Ibid., 4.
12. Ben Witherington III, *Making a Meal of It: Rethinking the Theology of the Lord's Supper* (Waco, TX: Baylor University Press, 2007), 23.
13. Brennan Manning, *The Ragamuffin Gospel: Good News for the Bedraggled, Beat-up, and Burnt Out* (Portland, OR: Multnomah Press, 1990), 59.
14. Pohl, *Making Room*, 6.
15. Perry, *Exploring the Evolution of the Lord's Supper in the New Testament*, 4.
16. Graydon Snyder, Julian Hills, and Richard Gardner, *Common Life in the Early Church* (Harrisburg, PA: Trinity Press International, 1998), 141. Serious scholars, such as N. T. Wright, question some of the conclusions of Crossan, the Jesus Seminar, and the work of the New Quest on the basis of good historical grounds. See N. T. Wright, *The Challenge of Jesus: Rediscovering Who Jesus Was and Is* (Downers Grove, IL: InterVarsity Press, 1999), 30.
17. Snyder, Hills, and Gardner, *Common Life in the Early Church*, 142.
18. Perry, *Exploring the Evolution of the Lord's Supper in the New Testament*, 9.
19. Snyder, Hills, and Gardner, *Common Life in the Early Church*, 141.
20. Perry, *Exploring the Evolution of the Lord's Supper in the New Testament*, 15.
21. Snyder, Hills, and Gardner, *Common Life in the Early Church*, 141.
22. Perry, *Exploring the Evolution of the Lord's Supper in the New Testament*, 9.
23. Ibid., 13.
24. Ibid., 12.
25. Ibid., 11.
26. Snyder, Hills, and Gardner, *Common Life in the Early Church*, 187.
27. Kenneth Leech, *Experiencing God: Theology as Spirituality*, 1st US ed. (San Francisco, CA: Harper & Row, 1985), 268.
28. Pohl, *Making Room*, 21–22.
29. Snyder, Hills, and Gardner, *Common Life in the Early Church*, 22.
30. Ibid., 23.
31. Ibid., 10.
32. Ibid., 14.
33. Pohl, *Making Room*, 74.
34. Snyder, Hills, and Gardner, *Common Life in the Early Church*, 60.
35. Elizabeth Newman, *Untamed Hospitality: Welcoming God and Other Strangers*, The Christian Practice of Everyday Life Series (Grand Rapids, MI: Brazos Press, 2007), 152.
36. Perry, *Exploring the Evolution of the Lord's Supper in the New Testament*, 2.
37. Ibid., 3.
38. Snyder, Hills, and Gardner, *Common Life in the Early Church*, 141.
39. Ralph P. Martin, *Worship in the Early Church*, rev. ed. (Grand Rapids, MI: Wm. B. Eerdmans Publishing Co., 1974), 122.

40. Snyder, Hills, and Gardner, *Common Life in the Early Church*, 88.
41. Perry, *Exploring the Evolution of the Lord's Supper in the New Testament*, v.
42. James F. White, *A Brief History of Christian Worship* (Nashville, TN: Abingdon Press, 1993), 26.
43. Michael Green, *Evangelism in the Early Church*, rev. ed. (Grand Rapids, MI: W. B. Eerdmans Publishing Co., 2004), 98.
44. Ibid., 319.
45. Tom Sine, *The New Conspirators: Creating the Future One Mustard Seed at a Time* (Downers Grove, IL: InterVarsity Press, 2008), 258.
46. Pohl, *Making Room*, 5.
47. Ibid., 106.
48. Ibid., 12.
49. Newman, *Untamed Hospitality*, 149.
50. Pohl, *Making Room*, 16.
51. Ibid., 130.
52. Ibid., 133.
53. Snyder, Hills, and Gardner, *Common Life in the Early Church*, 20.
54. Ibid., 200.
55. Pohl, *Making Room,* 33.
56. Perry, *Exploring the Evolution of the Lord's Supper in the New Testament*, 97.
57. Ibid., 40.
58. Snyder, Hills, and Gardner, *Common Life in the Early Church,* 89.
59. Pohl, *Making Room*, 41.
60. Snyder, Hills, and Gardner, *Common Life in the Early Church*, 133.
61. Pohl, *Making Room*, 32.
62. Ibid., 31.
63. E. A. Judge and David M. Scholer, *Social Distinctives of the Christians in the First Century: Pivotal Essays* (Peabody, MA: Hendrickson Publishers, 2008), 20.
64. Ibid.
65. Newman, *Untamed Hospitality,* 51.
66. Judge and Scholer, *Social Distinctives of the Christians in the First Century*, 25.
67. Robert J. Banks, *Paul's Idea of Community: The Early House Churches in Their Cultural Setting*, rev. ed. (Peabody, MA: Hendrickson Publishers, 1994), 35.
68. Newman, *Untamed Hospitality,* 53.
69. Ibid., 52.
70. Wayne A. Meeks, *The First Urban Christians: The Social World of the Apostle Paul*, 2nd ed. (New Haven, CT: Yale University Press, 2003), 77.
71. Snyder, Hills, and Gardner, *Common Life in the Early Church*, 65.
72. Maurice Simon, "Berakoth," http://www.come-and-hear.com/berakoth.
73. Sine, *The New Conspirators*, 63.
74. Meeks, *The First Urban Christians,* 79.

75. Ibid., 77.
76. Snyder, Hills, and Gardner, *Common Life in the Early Church,* 105–6.
77. Green, *Evanglism in the Early Church,* 255.
78. Witherington, *Making a Meal of It,* 105–6.
79. Green, *Evangelism in the Early Church,* 256.
80. Snyder, Hills, and Gardner, *Common Life in the Early Church,* 105.
81. Ibid., 106.
82. White, *A Brief History of Christian Worship,* 28.
83. Snyder, Hills, and Gardner, *Common Life in the Early Church,* 101.
84. Meeks, *The First Urban Christians,* 140.
85. Snyder, Hills, and Gardner, *Common Life in the Early Church,* 105.
86. Ibid.
87. Perry, *Exploring the Evaluation of the Lord's Supper in the New Testament,* 40.
88. Pohl, *Making Room,* 46.
89. Snyder, Hills, and Gardner, *Common Life in the Early Church,* 89.
90. Green, *Evangelism in the Early Church,* 256.
91. Alan Hirsch, *The Forgotten Ways: Reactivating the Missional Church* (Grand Rapids, MI: Brazos Press, 2006), 18.
92. Cheslyn Jones, *The Study of Liturgy,* rev. ed. (London: Oxford University Press, 1992), 211.
93. Dan Kimball, *Emerging Worship: Creating Worship Gatherings for New Generations* (Grand Rapids, MI: Zondervan, 2004), 95.
94. Snyder, Hills, and Gardner, *Common Life in the Early Church,* 107.
95. Ibid.
96. Ibid., 5.
97. White, *A Brief History of Christian Worship,* 42.
98. Snyder, Hills, and Gardner, *Common Life in the Early Church,* 112.
99. Ibid., 109.
100. Jones, *The Study of Liturgy,* 196.
101. Snyder, Hills, and Gardner, *Common Life in the Early Church,* 124.
102. Pohl, *Making Room,* 53.
103. Todd Eric Johnson, *The Conviction of Things Not Seen: Worship and Ministry in the 21st Century* (Grand Rapids, MI: Brazos Press, 2002), 31.
104. Paul Alexander, "The State of the Church" (lecture, Mattersay Hall, Mattersay, UK, March 1, 2010).
105. Werner O. Packull, *Hutterite Beginnings: Communitarian Experiments During the Reformation* (Baltimore, MD: Johns Hopkins University Press, 1995), 47.
106. Ibid., 44.
107. Ibid., 53.
108. Ibid., 62.
109. Ibid., 72.
110. Leanne Van Dyk, *A More Profound Alleluia: Theology and Worship in Harmony,* Calvin Institute of Christian Worship Liturgical Studies Series (Grand Rapids, MI: W. B. Eerdmans Publishing Co., 2005), 153.

111. White, *A Brief History of Christian Worship*, 26.
112. Pohl, *Making Room*, 23.
113. Ibid., 54.
114. Ibid.
115. Ibid., 55.
116. Ibid., 88.
117. J. Martin Bailey and Douglas R. Gilbert, *The Steps of Bonhoeffer: A Pictorial Album* (Philadelphia, PA: Pilgrim Press, 1969), 72.
118. Pohl, *Making Room*, 55.
119. Kimball, *Emerging Worship*, 82.
120. Johnson, *The Convictions of Things Not Seen*, 50.
121. Lesslie Newbigin, *The Gospel in a Pluralist Society* (Grand Rapids, MI: Wm. B. Eerdmans Publihsing Co., 1989), 95.
122. Pohl, *Making Room*, 35–36.
123. Ibid., 38.
124. Van Dyk, *A More Profound Alleluia*, 127.
125. Pohl, *Making Room*, 114.
126. Harold J. Westing, *Create and Celebrate Your Church's Uniqueness: Designing a Church Philosophy of Ministry* (Grand Rapids, MI: Kregel Publications, 1993), 156.
127. Avery Dulles, *Models of the Church*, exp. ed. (New York: Image Books, 2002), 144.
128. Marva J. Dawn, *Reaching Out without Dumbing Down: A Theology of Worship for the Turn-of-the-Century Culture* (Grand Rapids, MI: W. B. Eerdmans Publishing Co., 1995), 254.
129. David Kinnaman and Gabe Lyons, *Unchristian: What a New Generation Really Thinks about Christianity and Why It Matters* (Grand Rapids, MI: Baker Books, 2007), 35.
130. Snyder, Hills, and Gardner, *Common Life in the Early Church*, 120.
131. Ed Stetzer and David Putman, *Breaking the Missional Code: Your Church Can Become a Missionary in Your Community* (Nashville, TN: Broadman & Holman, 2006), 231.
132. Ibid.
133. Ibid.
134. Tim Dearborn and Scott Coil, *Worship at the Next Level: Insight from Contemporary Voices* (Grand Rapids, MI: Baker Books, 2004), 180–81.
135. George Barna, *The Frog in the Kettle: What Christians Need to Know about Life in the Year 2000* (Ventura, CA: Regal Books, 1990), 76.
136. Pohl, *Making Room*, 104.
137. Ibid., x.
138. Martin, *Worship in the Early Church*, 139–40.

Chapter 2: A Localized Apostolic Mind-Set

1. Alan Hirsch, *The Forgotten Ways: Reactivating the Missional Church* (Grand Rapids, MI: Brazos Press, 2006), 18.
2. Soong-Chan Rah, *The Next Evangelicalism: Releasing the Church from Western Cultural Captivity* (Downers Grove, IL: InterVarsity Press, 2009), 13.
3. Alan R. Johnson, *Apostolic Function in 21st Century Missions*, The J. Philip Hogan World Missions Series (Pasadena, CA: William Carey Library, 2009), 88.
4. Carol Alexander, "Postmodernism" (lecture, Mattersey Hall, UK, March 1, 2010).
5. Michael Frost and Alan Hirsch, *The Shaping of Things to Come: Innovation and Mission for the 21st-Century Church* (Peabody, MA: Hendrickson Publishers, 2003), 8.
6. Harold J. Westing, *Create and Celebrate Your Church's Uniqueness: Designing a Church Philosophy of Ministry* (Grand Rapids, MI: Kregel Publications, 1993), 157.
7. Daniel Tomberlin, *Encountering God at the Altar: The Sacraments in Pentecostal Worship* (Cleveland, TN: Pathway Press, 2006), 181.
8. Ed Stetzer, *Planting New Churches in a Postmodern Age* (Nashville, TN: Broadman & Holman, 2003), 24.
9. Jim Heugel, "Historical Christianity" (lecture, Northwest University, Kirkland, WA, February 16, 2011).
10. Paul Alexander, "The State of the Church" (lecture, Mattersey Hall, UK, March 1, 2010).
11. James Emery White, *Serious Times: Making Your Life Matter in an Urgent Day* (Downers Grove, IL: InterVarsity Press, 2004), 44.
12. David Olson, "16 Surprising Facts about the American Church," 24.
13. David Olson, *12 Surprising Facts about the American Church* (American Church Research Project, 2008), PowerPoint presentation, 38 frames, available at http://www.theamericanchurch.org, 25.
14. Frost and Hirsch, *The Shaping of Things to Come*, 18.
15. Stetzer, *Planting New Churches in a Postmodern Age*, 185.
16. Douglas J. Moo, *The Epistle to the Romans*, New International Commentary on the New Testament (Grand Rapids, MI: Wm. B. Eerdmans Publishing Co., 1996), 19.
17. William I. Gallaher (superintendent of the Assemblies of God, Oregon District), interview with the author, 1983.
18. Stetzer, *Planting New Churches in a Postmodern Age*, 7.
19. Hirsch, *The Forgotten Ways*, 151.
20. Rick Rusaw and Eric Swanson, *The Externally Focused Church* (Loveland, CO: Group Publishing, Inc., 2004), 188.
21. Ibid., 59.
22. Ibid., 171.

23. Darrell L. Guder et al., eds., *Missional Church: A Vision for the Sending of the Church in North America*, The Gospel and Our Culture Series (Grand Rapids, MI: W. B. Eerdmans Publishing Co., 1998), 6.
24. Johnson, *Apostolic Function in 21st Century Missions*, 170.
25. Guder et al., *Missional Church*, 44.
26. Hirsch, *The Forgotten Ways*, 158.
27. Frost and Hirsch, *The Shaping of Things to Come*, 172.
28. Ibid., 179.
29. Hirsch, *The Forgotten Ways*, 161, 166.
30. Darrell L. Guder, *The Continuing Conversion of the Church*, The Gospel and Our Culture Series (Grand Rapids, MI: W. B. Eerdmans Publishing Co., 2000), 71.
31. Will Mancini, *Church Unique: How Missional Leaders Cast Vision, Capture Culture, and Create Movement* (San Francisco, CA: Jossey-Bass, 2008), 95.
32. Hirsch, *The Forgotten Ways*, 154.
33. Michael Green, *Evangelism in the Early Church*, rev. ed. (Grand Rapids, MI: W. B. Eerdmans Publishing Co., 2004), 15.
34. Daniel Tomberlin, *Pentecostal Sacraments: Encountering God at the Altar* (Cleveland, TN: Center for Pentecostal Leadership & Care, 2010), 18.
35. Hirsch, *The Forgotten Ways*, 78.
36. Andy Stanley, *The Next Generation Leader: 5 Essentials for Those Who Will Shape the Future* (Sisters, OR: Multnomah Press, 2003), 31.
37. Johnson, *Apostolic Function in 21st Century Missions*, 51.
38. Ibid., 65.
39. Hirsch, *The Forgotten Ways*, 20.
40. Johnson, *Apostolic Function in 21st Century Missions*, 78.
41. Ibid., 77.
42. Green, *Evangelism in the Early Church*, 167.
43. Johnson, *Apostolic Function in 21st Century Missions*, 98.
44. Ibid., 96.
45. Ibid., 98.
46. Ibid., 99.
47. Ibid., 46.
48. Todd Eric Johnson, *The Conviction of Things Not Seen: Worship and Ministry in the 21st Century* (Grand Rapids, MI: Brazos Press, 2002), 187.
49. Green, *Evangelism in the Early Church*, 98.
50. Johnson, *The Conviction of Things Not Seen*, 187.
51. Myron B. Penner, ed., *Christianity and the Postmodern Turn: Six Views* (Grand Rapids, MI: Brazos Press, 2005), 150.
52. David Lim, *Spiritual Gifts: A Fresh Look* (Springfield, MO: Gospel Publishing House, 1991), 101.
53. Robert C. Anderson, *Circles of Influence* (Chicago, IL: Moody Press, 1991), 107.
54. Johnson, *Apostolic Function in 21st Century Missions*, 22.

55. Guder et al., *Missional Church*, 3.
56. Guder, *The Continuing Conversion of the Church*, 19.
57. Guder et al., *Missional Church*, 85.
58. Ibid., 81.
59. Johnson, *Apostolic Function in 21st Century Missions*, 171.
60. Ibid., 174.
61. Lesslie Newbigin, *The Gospel in a Pluralist Society* (Grand Rapids, MI: W. B. Eerdmans Publishing Co., 1989), 231.
62. Johnson, *Apostolic Function in 21st Century Missions*, 172.
63. Stetzer, *Planting New Churches in a Postmodern Age*, 246.
64. Ibid., 247.
65. Ibid., 246.
66. Ray Sherman Anderson, *The Shape of Practical Theology: Empowering Ministry with Theological Praxis* (Downers Grove, IL: InterVarsity Press, 2001), 32.
67. Tom Sine, *The New Conspirators: Creating the Future One Mustard Seed at a Time* (Downers Grove, IL: InterVarsity Press, 2008), 193.
68. Lyle E. Schaller, *The Change Agent* (Nashville, TN: Abingdon Press, 1972), 50.
69. James K. A. Smith, *Who's Afraid of Postmodernism?: Taking Derrida, Lyotard, and Foucault to Church*, The Church and Postmodern Culture Series (Grand Rapids, MI: Baker Academic, 2006), 143.
70. George Barna, *The Frog in the Kettle: What Christians Need to Know about Life in the Year 2000* (Ventura, CA: Regal Books, 1990), 195.
71. Green, *Evangelism in the Early Church*, 23–24.
72. White, *Serious Times*, 144.
73. Christine D. Pohl, *Making Room: Recovering Hospitality as a Christian Tradition* (Grand Rapids, MI: W. B. Eerdmans Publishing Co., 1999), 111.
74. Ibid., 55.
75. Ibid., 159.
76. Johnson, *Apostolic Function in 21st Century Missions*, 153.
77. Ibid., 128.
78. Ibid., 152.
79. Smith, *Who's Afraid of Postmodernism?*, 142.
80. David Lim, *The Drama of Redemption* (Singapore: OneStoneBooks, 2008), 63.
81. Leonard I. Sweet and Edward H. Hammett, *The Gospel According to Starbucks: Living with a Grande Passion* (Colorado Springs, CO: Waterbrook Press, 2007), 132.
82. Leanne Van Dyk, ed., *A More Profound Alleluia: Theology and Worship in Harmony*, Calvin Institute of Christian Worship Liturgical Studies Series (Grand Rapids, MI: W. B. Eerdmans Publishing Co., 2005), 127.
83. Ed Stetzer and David Putman, *Breaking the Missional Code: Your Church Can Become a Missionary in Your Community* (Nashville, TN: Broadman & Holman, 2006), 163.
84. Rah, *The Next Evangelicalism*, 191.

85. Johnson, *Apostolic Function in 21st Century Missions*, 101.

86. Ibid., 160.

Chapter 3: Organic Approaches

1. Aubrey Malphurs, *Advanced Strategic Planning: A New Model for Church and Ministry Leaders*, 2nd ed. (Grand Rapids, MI: Baker Books, 2005), 8.

2. Reggie McNeal, *Missional Renaissance: Changing the Scorecard for the Church* (San Francisco, CA: Jossey-Bass, 2009), 62.

3. Alton Garrison, *Hope in American Crisis* (Springfield, MO: Gospel Publishing House, 2007), 40.

4. Malphurs, *Advanced Strategic Planning*, 77.

5. Neil Cole, *Organic Church: Growing Faith Where Life Happens* (San Francisco, CA: Jossey-Bass, 2005).

6. Thom S. Rainer and Eric Geiger, *Simple Church: Returning to God's Process for Making Disciples* (Nashville, TN: Broadman Press, 2006).

7. Dave Ferguson, Jon Ferguson, and Eric Bramlett, *The Big Idea: Focus the Message, Multiply the Impact*, the Leadership Network Innovation Series (Grand Rapids, MI: Zondervan, 2007).

8. Soong-Chan Rah, *The Next Evangelicalism: Releasing the Church from Western Cultural Captivity* (Downers Grove, IL: InterVarsity Press, 2009), 100.

9. Ibid., 104.

10. Ibid., 113.

11. Ibid.

12. Ibid., 104.

13. Mark Driscoll, *Confessions of a Reformission Rev.: Hard Lessons from an Emerging Missional Church*, the Leadership Network Innovation Series (Grand Rapids, MI: Zondervan, 2006), 93.

14. Ibid.

15. Rah, *The Next Evangelicalism*, 105.

16. Ibid., 106.

17. Garrison, *Hope in America's Crisis*, 11.

18. Ibid., 41.

19. Warren G. Bennis, Gretchen M. Spreitzer, and Thomas G. Cummings, *The Future of Leadership: Today's Top Leadership Thinkers Speak to Tomorrow's Leaders*, the Jossey-Bass Business & Management Series (San Francisco, CA: Jossey-Bass, 2001), 3.

20. Ron McManus, "The Transformational Church" (lecture, Assemblies of God Theological Seminary, Springfield, MO, March 2009).

21. Malphurs, *Advanced Strategic Planning*, 123.

22. Ibid., 34.

23. Ibid., 72.

24. James C. Collins, *Good to Great: Why Some Companies Make the Leap and Others Don't* (New York: HarperBusiness, 2001), 14.
25. The church staff of St. Aldates, Oxford, UK, interview by the author, March 2012.
26. Waldemar Kowalski, "The Book of Romans" (lecture, Northwest University, Kirkland, WA, March 22, 2010).
27. Ron Martoia, *Transformational Architecture: Reshaping Our Lives as Narrative* (Grand Rapids, MI: Zondervan, 2008), 174.
28. Dan Kimball, *Emerging Worship: Creating Worship Gatherings for New Generations* (Grand Rapids, MI: Zondervan, 2004), 32.
29. Leith Anderson, *A Church for the 21st Century* (Minneapolis, MN: Bethany House Publishers, 1992), 128.
30. Leonard I. Sweet and Andy Crouch, *The Church in Emerging Culture: Five Perspectives* (El Cajon, CA: Youth Specialties, 2003), 194.
31. Daniel Tomberlin, *Pentecostal Sacraments: Encountering God at the Altar* (Cleveland, TN: Center for Pentecostal Leadership & Care, 2010), 2.
32. Reggie McNeal, *Missional Renaissance: Changing the Scorecard for the Church* (San Francisco, CA: Jossey-Bass, 2009), 11.
33. Bennis, Spreitzer, and Cummings, *The Future of Leadership*, 256. Actually stated as "winning a victory for humanity."

Chapter 4: Calling Forth Mission-Based Christians

1. John Dyer, *From the Garden to the City: The Redeeming and Corrupting Power of Technology* (Grand Rapids, MI: Kregel Publications, 2011), 35.
2. Jim Heugel, "Historical Theology" (lecture, Northwest University, Kirkland, WA, February 16, 2011).
3. Alton Garrison, *Hope in America's Crisis* (Springfield, MO: Gospel Publishing House, 2007), 34.
4. Dan Kimball, *They Like Jesus but Not the Church: Insights from Emerging Generations* (Grand Rapids, MI: Zondervan, 2007), 37.
5. Deborah Ancona and Henrik Bresman, *X-Teams* (Boston, MA: Harvard Business School Press, 2007), 81.
6. Garrison, *Hope in America's Crisis*, 40.
7. Roger Heuser, "Soul Care" (lecture, Northwest University, Kirkland, WA, October 22, 2012).
8. Steve Mills, "Life Cycle of a Church" (lecture, Bethany Christian Assembly, Everett, WA, May 2003).
9. Michael Green, *Evangelism in the Early Church*, rev. ed. (Grand Rapids, MI: W. B. Eerdmans Publishing Co., 2004), 12.
10. Alan R. Johnson, *Apostolic Function in 21st Century Missions*, The J. Philip Hogan World Missions Series (Pasadena, CA: William Carey Library, 2009), 98.

11. Darrell L. Guder, *The Continuing Conversion of the Church*, the Gospel and Our Culture Series (Grand Rapids, MI: W. B. Eerdmans Publishing Co., 2000), 120.

12. David Lim, *The Drama of Redemption* (Singapore: OneStoneBooks, 2008), 143.

13. Graydon Snyder, Julian Hills, and Richard Gardner, *Common Life in the Early Church* (Harrisburg, PA: Trinity Press International, 1998), 187.

14. Ed Stetzer, *Planting New Churches in a Postmodern Age* (Nashville, TN: Broadman & Holman, 2003), 10.

15. John Bueno, *An Open Heart* (Springfield, MO: Gospel Publishing House, 2007), 87.

16. David Godwin, interview with author, April 1992.

17. Kilian McDonnel and George Montague, *Christian Initiation and Baptism in the Holy Spirit: Evidence from the First Eight Centuries* (Collegeville, MN: Liturgical Press, 1994), 72.

18. David Lim, "Holy Spirit in the Church" (lecture, Orlando, FL, June 23, 2010).

19. Ibid.

20. An overview of the book of Acts reveals four clear instances of tongues, five instances of divine visions, fourteen instances of empowered speaking, and twenty-three instances of healings, signs, and wonders.

21. Snyder, Hills, and Gardner, *Common Life in the Early Church*, 141.

22. Miroslav Volf, *Exclusion and Embrace: A Theological Exploration of Identity, Otherness, and Reconciliation* (Nashville, TN: Abingdon Press, 1996).

23. Guder, *The Continuing Conversion of the Church*, 93–94.

24. Aubrey Malphurs, *Advanced Strategic Planning: A New Model for Church and Ministry Leaders*, 2nd ed. (Grand Rapids, MI: Baker Books, 2005), 8.

25. Edgar Schein, *Organizational Culture and Leadership* (San Francisco, CA: Jossey-Bass, 2004), 11.

26. Jeffrey Sonnenfeld, "Historic Leadership's Greatest Battle: The Defeat of Disappointment Versus the Disappointment of Defeat," in *The Future of Leadership: Today's Top Leadership Thinkers Speak to Tomorrow's Leaders*, the Jossey-Bass Business & Management Series, eds. Warren G. Bennis, Gretchen M. Spreitzer, and Thomas G. Cummings (San Francisco, CA: Jossey-Bass, 2001), 185.

27. Rob Ketterling, "His Story" (lecture, Coeur d'Alene, ID, April 24, 2013).

28. Malphurs, *Advanced Strategic Planning*, 70.

29. John P. Kotter, *Leading Change* (Boston, MA: Harvard Business Review Press, 2012), 42–43.

30. James C. Collins, *Good to Great: Why Some Companies Make the Leap and Others Don't* (New York: HarperBusiness, 2001), 114, 116.

31. Ibid., 13.

Chapter 5: Preferring the Poor

1. Bill O'Reilly, *The O' Reilly Factor*, aired April 2013.
2. United States Census Bureau, "Selected Economic Characteristics: 2005–2009: Seattle city, Washington," American Factfinder, http://factfinder.census.gov/servlet/ADPTable?_bm=y&-geo_id=16000US5363000&-qr_name=ACS_2009_5YR_G00_DP5YR3&-ds_name=ACS_2009_5YR_G00_&-_lang=en&-_sse=on.
3. Philip Yancey, *Church, Why Bother? My Personal Pilgrimage, Growing Deeper* (Grand Rapids, MI: Zondervan, 1998), 32.
4. Christine D. Pohl, *Making Room: Recovering Hospitality as a Christian Tradition* (Grand Rapids, MI: W. B. Eerdmans Publishing Co., 1999), 11–12.
5. Ibid., 15.
6. Yancey, *Church, Why Bother?*, 45.
7. Earl Creps, *Off-Road Disciplines: Spiritual Adventures of Missional Leaders* (San Francisco, CA: Jossey-Bass, 2006), 93.
8. Alan R. Johnson, *Apostolic Function in 21st Century Missions*, The J. Philip Hogan World Missions Series (Pasadena, CA: William Carey Library, 2009), 22.
9. Thomas Merton, *No Man Is an Island*, 1st Shambhala ed. (Boston, MA: Shambhala Publications, 2005), 21.
10. James Emery White, *Serious Times: Making Your Life Matter in an Urgent Day* (Downers Grove, IL: InterVarsity Press, 2004), 144.
11. Charles W. Colson and Harold Fickett, *The Faith: What Christians Believe, Why They Believe It, and Why It Matters* (Grand Rapids, MI: Zondervan, 2008), 15.
12. Ibid., 17.
13. David Kinnaman and Gabe Lyons, *Unchristian: What a New Generation Really Thinks about Christianity and Why It Matters* (Grand Rapids, MI: Baker Books, 2007), 87.
14. Pohl, *Making Room*, 98.
15. Ibid., 88.
16. Colson and Fickett, *The Faith*, 169.
17. Geoff Pickup (lecture to MA class, Derbe, UK, March 3, 2010).
18. M. Rex Miller, *The Millennium Matrix: Reclaiming the Past, Reframing the Future of the Church* (San Francisco, CA: Jossey-Bass, 2004), 126.
19. Todd Eric Johnson, *The Conviction of Things Not Seen: Worship and Ministry in the 21st Century* (Grand Rapids, MI: Brazos Press, 2002), 114.
20. Abraham Maslow, *Maslow Hierarchy of Needs* (blog), accessed December 6, 2016, http://www.Abraham-Maslow.com/m_motivation/Hierarchy_of_Needs.asp.
21. Rick Rusaw and Eric Swanson, *The Externally Focused Church* (Loveland, CO: Group Publishing, 2004), 118.

22. Leith Anderson, *A Church for the 21st Century* (Minneapolis, MN: Bethany House Publishers, 1992), 226.

23. Lewis Shelton, interview by author, November 8, 2012.

24. Jessie Willis, "How We Measure Poverty: A History and Brief Overview," Oregon Center for Public Policy, February 2000, http://www.ocpp.org /poverty/how.htm#1a.

25. Ibid.

26. Ibid.

27. U.S. Census Bureau, "Selected Economic Characteristics: 2005–2009: Seattle city, Washington."

28. Committee to End Homelessness, "Scope of the Problem (Seattle) 2010," http://www.cehkc.org/scope/causes.aspx, no longer accessible.

29. Ibid.

30. C. Smith and P. Nyhan, "Surprising Face of Working Poor: Their Jobs Allow Them to Barely Hang On in City—and They're All Around," *Seattle Post-Intelligencer*, February 15, 2006, http://www.seattlepi.com /local/259649_pooroverview16.html.

31. Lyle E. Schaller, *The Change Agent* (Nashville, TN: Abingdon Press, 1972), 33.

32. Tom Sine, *The New Conspirators: Creating the Future One Mustard Seed at a Time* (Downers Grove, IL: InterVarsity Press, 2008), 180.

33. Ibid., 66.

34. Ibid., 175.

35. Richard Stearns, *The Hole in Our Gospel: What Does God Expect of Us? The Answer That Changed My Life and Might Just Change the World*, large print ed. (Waterville, ME: Christian Large Print, 2010), 95.

36. Soong-Chan Rah, *The Next Evangelicalism: Releasing the Church from Western Cultural Captivity* (Downers Grove, IL: InterVarsity Press, 2009), 41.

37. Ibid., 51.

38. Stearns, *The Hole in Our Gospel*, 104.

39. Ibid., 158.

40. Ibid., 218.

41. Ibid., 219.

42. Wonsuk Ma, "The Shelf Life of World Christianity" (lecture, Oxford Center of Mission Studies, Oxford, UK, March 2, 2010).

43. Geoff Pickup, interview with author, March 2010.

44. Randy Walls, "The Bell Curve of Adoption" (lecture, Northwest University, Kirkland, WA, October 2006).

45. Alton Garrison, *Hope in America's Crisis* (Springield, MO: Gospel Publishing House, 2007), 123.

46. Jean Vanier, *Community and Growth* (Mahwah, NJ: Paulist Press, 1989), 63.

47. Merton, *No Man Is an Island*, 74.

Chapter 6: A Neighborhood Vision

1. John Dyer, *From the Garden to the City: The Redeeming and Corrupting Power of Technology* (Grand Rapids, MI: Kregel Publications, 2011), 91.
2. Marva J. Dawn, *Reaching Out without Dumbing Down: A Theology of Worship for the Turn-of-the-Century Culture* (Grand Rapids, MI: W. B. Eerdmans Publishing Co., 1995), 26.
3. Peter Katz. *The New Urbanism: Toward an Architecture of Community* (San Francisco, CA: McGraw-Hill, 1994), xviii.
4. Leonard I. Sweet and Edward H. Hammett, *The Gospel According to Starbucks: Living with a Grande Passion* (Colorado Springs, CO: Waterbrook Press, 2007), 105.
5. George Barna, *The Frog in the Kettle: What Christians Need to Know about Life in the Year 2000* (Ventura, CA: Regal Books, 1990), 76.
6. Reggie McNeal, *Missional Renaissance: Changing the Scorecard for the Church* (San Francisco, CA: Jossey-Bass, 2009), 50.
7. Geoff Surratt, Greg Ligon, and Warren Bird, *The Multi-Site Church Revolution: Being One Church in Many Locations*, the Leadership Network Innovation Series (Grand Rapids, MI: Zondervan, 2006), 65.
8. Soong-Chan Rah, *The Next Evangelicalism: Releasing the Church from Western Cultural Captivity* (Downers Grove, IL: InterVarsity Press, 2009), 152.
9. James Emery White, *Serious Times: Making Your Life Matter in an Urgent Day* (Downers Grove, IL: InterVarsity Press, 2004), 158.
10. Rah, *The Next Evangelicalism*, 148.
11. Alan J. Roxburgh, M. Scott Boren, and Mark Priddy, *Introducing the Missional Church: What It Is, Why It Matters, How to Become One*, Allelon Missional Series (Grand Rapids, MI: Baker Books, 2009), 89.
12. Tom Sine, *The New Conspirators: Creating the Future One Mustard Seed at a Time* (Downers Grove, IL: InterVarsity Press, 2008), 193.
13. Roxburgh, Boren, and Priddy, *Introducing the Missional Church*, 94.
14. Ibid., 54.

Chapter 7: Funding Streams

1. Mark Batterson, *In the Pit with a Lion on a Snowy Day: How to Survive and Thrive When Opportunity Roars* (New York: MJF Books, 2012), 59.
2. Ed Stetzer and David Putman, *Breaking the Missional Code: Your Church Can Become a Missionary in Your Community* (Nashville, TN: Broadman & Holman, 2006), 163.
3. Rick Rusaw and Eric Swanson, *The Externally Focused Church* (Loveland, CO: Group Publishing, Inc., 2004), 188.
4. Ed Stetzer, *Planting New Churches in a Postmodern Age* (Nashville, TN: Broadman & Holman, 2003), 247.

5. M. Rex Miller, *The Millennium Matrix: Reclaiming the Past, Reframing the Future of the Church* (San Francisco, CA: Jossey-Bass, 2004), 125.
6. Philip Yancey, *Church, Why Bother? My Personal Pilgrimage, Growing Deeper* (Grand Rapids, MI, Zondervan, 1998), 33.
7. Christine Pohl, *Making Room: Recovering Hospitality as a Christian Tradition* (Grand Rapids; MI: Wm. B. Eerdmans Publishing Co., 1999), 88.
8. Bob Rose (secretary-treasurer of the Oregon District of the AG), lecture to Oregon Ministers Meeting, 1983.
9. Harold J. Westing, *Create and Celebrate Your Church's Uniqueness: Designing a Church Philosophy of Ministry* (Grand Rapids, MI: Kregel Publications, 1993).

Conclusion

1. Bill O'Reilly, *The O' Reilly Factor*, aired April 2013.
2. United States Census Bureau, "Selected Economic Characteristics: 2005–2009: Seattle city, Washington," American Factfinder, http://factfinder .census.gov/servlet/ADPTable?_bm=y&-geo_id=16000US5363000&-qr _name=ACS_2009_5YR_G00_DP5YR3&-ds_name=ACS_2009_5YR_G00 _&-_lang=en&-_sse=on.
3. Philip Yancey, *Church, Why Bother? My Personal Pilgrimage, Growing Deeper* (Grand Rapids, MI: Zondervan, 1998), 32.
4. Earl G. Creps, *Off-Road Disciplines: Spiritual Adventures of Missional Leaders* (San Francisco, CA: Jossey-Bass, 2006), 93.
5. Michael Green, *Evangelism in the Early Church* (Grand Rapids, MI: Wm. B. Eerdmans Publishing Co., 2003), 318; Ben Witherington III, *Making a Meal of It: Rethinking the Theology of the Lord's Supper* (Waco, TX: Baylor University Press, 2007), 101.

Appendix D

1. Jim Cymbala, "It Is Time to Change Something" (lecture, Orlando, FL, August 6, 2013).

ABOUT THE AUTHOR

Dr. Verlon and Melodee Fosner have led a multi-site dinner church in Seattle, Washington, since 1999 (www.CommunityDinners.com). In 2014 they founded the Dinner Church Collective (www.DinnerChurchCollective.net), which is a church-planting network centered on Jesus' dinner church theology. In this decade, when more churches in the United States are declining than thriving, and when eighty churches a week are closing, Verlon and Melodee sensed that a different way of doing church was needed for their ninety-three-year-old Seattle congregation. It soon became obvious that they were not the only ones in need of a different path. There is a lot to be gained when church leaders begin to see open doors in the American landscape that they had previously overlooked. Therein lies the journey for those who will forge a new future for the American church.

The Fosners have three adult children all of whom are married and bringing on the next generation, which for now means five grandchildren.

CPSIA information can be obtained
at www.ICGtesting.com
Printed in the USA
LVHW020310240623
750317LV00002B/5